T H E
Elements of Grammar

OTHER PAPERBACK TITLES OF INTEREST

The Elements of Editing
Arthur Plotnik

The Elements of Correspondence
Mary A. De Vries

The Elements of Speechwriting and Public Speaking
Jeff Scott Cook

The Elements of Business Writing
Gary Blake and Robert W. Bly

The Elements of Legal Writing
Martha Faulk and Irving M. Mehler

The Elements of Nonsexist Usage
Val Dumond

The Elements of Technical Writing
Gary Blake and Robert W. Bly

The Elements of Screenwriting
Irwin R. Blacker

The Elements of Playwriting
Louis. E. Catron

The Art of Questioning
Peter Megargee Brown

*How to Write a Children's Book and
Get It Published*
Barbara Seuling

T H E
Elements of Grammar

Margaret D. Shertzer

MACMILLAN • USA

Macmillan General Reference
A Simon & Schuster Macmillan Company
1633 Broadway
New York, NY 10019-6785

Based on *The Secretary's Handbook* by Sarah Augusta
Taintor and Kate M. Monro

Library of Congress Cataloging-in-Publication Data
Shertzer, Margaret D.
    The elements of grammar / Margaret D. Shertzer.
        p.   cm.
    Includes bibliographical references and index.
    ISBN 0-02-861449-6 (pbk.)
    1. English language—Grammar—Handbooks, manuals, etc.
I. Title.
PE1112.S54   1996
428.2—dc20   96-3007
                                                  CIP

10   9   8   7   6   5   4

Printed in the United States of America

Contents

THE
Elements of Grammar

CHAPTER ONE

Recognizing Good Grammar

Grammar may be defined as a system of rules for the use of language, or as a study of what is preferred and what is to be avoided in effective speech and writing.

We all speak and write whether or not we are able to state rules governing the words we use. To be effective we must achieve clarity of expression. We need to know how to present ideas forcefully, without confusion or unnecessary words, by choosing language suited to our purpose.

A speaker may say, "It's me. I ain't the one that come first, but I'm gonna speak for all us boys." The intent is clear, but the choice of words is crude. While informal speech commonly uses colloquial expressions, few people wish to appear illiterate in their speaking or writing.

In order to use English correctly and gracefully, it is necessary to recognize and to practice using good grammar. Listening to speakers who are accustomed to speaking grammatically helps to train the ear to recognize correct usage. Simple, idiomatic English is desirable for both writing and speaking, but it is not effortless.

Good habits of speech will improve one's writing, but the best training may be to read examples of effective writing. Whether the subject is a news report, a humorous anecdote, a comment on today's events, a description of an exciting happening, or a romantic novel—any of these kinds of writing can be satisfying to read and instructive to study. The following are examples of various styles of

1

English composition, each the work of a writer who has mastered his craft.

. . . To regard the people of any time as particularly obtuse seems vaguely improper, and it also establishes a precedent which members of this generation might regret. Yet it seems certain that the economists and those who offered economic counsel in the late twenties and early thirties were almost uniquely perverse. In the months and years following the stock market crash, the burden of reputable economic advice was invariably on the side of measures that would make things worse.

JOHN KENNETH GALBRAITH, *The Great Crash 1929*

Big money in turn has brought big emotional trouble. Envy is the new worm in the apple of sport. To read about the New York Yankees as they bickered through the summer of 1977, when Reggie Jackson had arrived toting his monetary bundle, was like reading Ann Landers. The game was secondary; first we had to learn whose feelings were hurt, whose pride was wounded. In once-sedate tennis, the pot of gold is now enormous and the players are strung as tightly as their rackets. In football and basketball the pay is sky-high, and so is the umbrage.

WILLIAM ZINSSER, *On Writing Well*

. . . Dick goes out on the leveled stream and lays down harnesses in the snow. The sled is packed, the gear lashed under skins. Everything is ready for the dogs. They are barking, roaring, screaming with impatience for the run. One by one, Donna unchains them. Out of the trees they dash toward the sled. Chipper goes first and, standing in front, holds all the harnesses in a good taut line. Abie, Little Girl, Grandma, Ug—the others fast fill in. They jump in their traces, can't wait to go. If they jump too much, they get cuffed. Wait another minute and they'll have everything so twisted we'll be here another hour. Go! The whole team hits at once. The sled, which was at rest a moment before, is moving fast. Destination, Eagle; time, two days.

JOHN MCPHEE, *Coming into the Country*

A good laboratory, like a good bank or a corporation or government, has to run like a computer. Almost everything is done flawlessly, by the book, and all the numbers add up to the predicted sums. The days go by. And then, if it is a lucky day, and a lucky laboratory, somebody makes a mistake; the wrong buffer, something in one of the blanks, a decimal misplaced in reading counts, the warm room off by a degree and a half, a mouse out of his box, or just a misreading of the day's protocol. Whatever, when the results come in, something is obviously screwed up, and then the action can begin.

The misreading is not the important error; it opens the way. The next step is the crucial one. If the investigator can bring himself to say, "But even so, look at that!" then the new finding, whatever it is, is ready for snatching. What is needed, for progress to be made, is the move based on the error.

LEWIS THOMAS, *The Medusa and the Snail*

CHAPTER TWO

Some Grammatical Terms

The terms used in grammar help to explain the function and relationship of the words in sentences.

1. A *noun* is the name of a person, place, thing, or idea. Common nouns refer to any person, place, thing, idea, etc.

   boy   house   water   town   religion   despair

   Proper nouns refer to particular places, persons, objects, ideas, etc.

   George   the White House   Yokohama   Christian Science

   Nouns are used as the subjects of sentences, and as the objects of verbs and prepositions. (*See also* Recognition of the Subject, pp. 22–25, and Agreement of Adjective and Noun, pp. 39–40.)

2. A *pronoun* can take the place of a noun.

   John called *his* mother as soon as *he* returned from work.
   The cat sat by *her* dish, waiting to be fed.

   (*See* Pronouns, pp. 14–22.)

3. *Case* refers to the form of a noun or pronoun which shows its relationship to other words in a sentence. In English there are three cases: nominative (used for the subject of the sentence or clause), possessive (showing who owns something), and objective (receiving the action of the verb or preposition). Nouns do not change their form except in the possessive case, when *'s* is

added. Pronouns have different forms for each case. (*See* Pronouns, pp. 14–22.)

4. A *verb* shows the action or state of being, and it also indicates the time of action or being.

He *waived* his right to appeal. (past)
I *need* your report now. (present)
You *will enjoy* your trip to Norway. (future)

(*See* Verbs, pp. 22–35.)

5. *Adjectives* are words that describe nouns and specify size, color, number, and the like. This quality is called modifying, and an adjective is a modifier.

A *small* light showed in an *upper* window of the *old* factory.
The *two old* ladies lived in the *big stone* house.

(*See* Adjectives and Adverbs, pp. 35–41.)

6. *Adverbs* are words that describe verbs, adjectives, and other adverbs. They specify in what manner, when, where, and how much.

The child screamed *loudly* as the doctor prepared an injection.
It is *much* later than I thought.

(*See* Adjectives and Adverbs, pp. 35–41.)

7. *Prepositions* show how a noun or pronoun is related to another word in a sentence.

The dog came bounding *into* the room.
He parked *behind* the truck.
In this instance, I believe you are mistaken.

When used with a verb, the combination of verb and preposition usually has a meaning different from the verb alone.

They *laughed at* the very idea.
I must *look into* the proposal before I decide.
Have you *come to* any conclusion?

(*See* Prepositions, pp. 41–44.)

8. *Conjunctions* join words, phrases, or clauses. Coordinating conjunctions connect sentence elements of the same value; single words, phrases, or clauses. These conjunctions are *and, but, for, or, nor, either, neither, yet, so,* and *so that.* (*Yet* and *so* are also used as adverbs.)

Subordinating conjunctions join two clauses, the main one and the dependent (or subordinate) one. The conjunctions used with dependent clauses are: *although, because, since, until, while,* and others which place a condition on the sentence. (*See* Conjunctions, pp. 45–46, and Subordinate Clauses, pp. 46–47.)

The Parts of a Sentence

1. *Subject and predicate.* A sentence expresses a complete thought and consists of a subject and a predicate. (If either the subject or predicate is not expressed, it must be readily understood from sentences that precede or follow.)

The subject of a sentence is the person, object, or idea being described. The predicate is the explanation of the action, condition, or effect of the subject.

The after-Christmas sale is nearly over.
Getting a job can be a difficult process.

In the examples above, the subjects are in italics; the rest of the sentences are the predicates.

Subjects are nouns, pronouns, or phrases used as nouns. Predicates are verbs and the words used to explain the action or condition. (*See* Recognition of the Subject, pp. 22–25.)

2. *Phrases.* A phrase is a group of words that are closely related but have no subject or predicate. A phrase may be used as a noun, verb, adjective, or adverb.

Noun: *Waiting for a telephone call* has kept me at home all morning.
Verb: That work *could have been done* earlier.

Adjective: The building *with the satellite dish on the roof* has been converted to a condominium.
Adverb: The price is higher *out of season.*

A phrase that is essential to the meaning of the sentence is called restrictive. A phrase which is actually a parenthetical comment is called nonrestrictive and is usually set off by commas.

Restrictive: The computer *in my office* is used *by several people.*
Nonrestrictive: I wonder, *by the way,* who will be named director.

(*See* Prepositions, pp. 41–44.)

3. Clauses. A clause is a group of words which has a subject and a predicate. A main clause can stand alone as a sentence. A subordinate clause is incomplete and is used with a main clause to express a related idea.

Main Clause: *This is the man who sold me the dog.*
I enjoy walking our dog when the weather is good.
Subordinate Clause: I enjoy walking our dog, *which we bought last week.*
When I have time, I like to work out at the gym.

(*See* Relative Pronouns, pp. 18–19; Correlative Conjunctions, pp. 45–46; Subordinate Conjunctions, p. 46; and Subordinate Clauses, pp. 46–47.)

CHAPTER THREE

Points of Grammar

Formation of Noun Plurals

1. Most nouns form the plural by adding *s* to the singular.

banks	chemists	hospitals	letters

2. Nouns ending in *f, fe,* and *ff*:

(1) Some nouns ending in *f, fe,* and *ff* form their plurals regularly by adding *s* to the singular.

briefs	giraffes	proofs	sheriffs
chiefs	plaintiffs	scarfs	tariffs

(2) Some nouns ending in *f* and *fe* change these letters to *v* and add *es* to form the plural.

halves	leaves	selves	thieves
knives	lives	shelves	wives'

3. Common nouns ending in *s, sh, ch, x,* and *z* form their plurals by adding *es* to the singular if an extra syllable is needed in pronouncing the plural

annexes	churches	lunches	waltzes
brushes	dishes	quartzes	waxes
businesses	dispatches	sixes	witnesses
chintzes	hoaxes	taxes	yeses

But: buses *or* busses

4. Nouns ending in *y:*

(1) Nouns ending in *y* preceded by a consonant form their plurals by changing *y* to *i* and adding *es.*

armies	diaries	families	quantities
authorities	discoveries	industries	skies
cities	duties	ladies	utilities
companies	fallacies	parties	vacancies

(2) Nouns ending in *y* preceded by a vowel, except those ending in *quy,* form their plurals in the usual way by adding *s* to the singular.

attorneys	journeys	keys	valleys

5. Nouns ending in *o* form their plurals by adding *s* or *es,* but there are many exceptions and alternatives to the following generalizations so that it is advisable to consult a dictionary when in doubt.

(1) Most common nouns ending in *o* preceded by a vowel form their plurals by adding *s* to the singular.

cameos	patios	radios	rodeos
curios	portfolios	ratios	studios

(2) Most common nouns ending in *o* preceded by a consonant form their plurals by adding *es* to the singular.

embargoes	manifestoes	noes	vetoes
heroes	Negroes	torpedoes	

But: cantos, pianos, solos, sopranos, tobaccos

(3) Some nouns ending in *o* form their plurals by adding either *s* or *es* to the singular.

cargos *or*	mottos *or* mottoes	provisos *or*
cargoes	mulattos *or*	provisoes
manifestos *or*	mulattoes	zero *or*
manifestoes		zeros

6. Some nouns form their plurals by a change in an internal vowel.

feet   geese   men   mice   teeth   women

7. Some nouns have the same form in the plural as in the singular.

aircraft	deer	salmon
chassis	grass	series
corps	moose	sheep

Some of these nouns are pluralized when they represent several species.

the deers of North America   grasses found on the prairies

8. Some nouns are always plural. They have no singular form in the same sense.

annals	earnings	scales
assets	goods	scissors
auspices	headquarters	trousers
ceramics	pants	
credentials	proceeds	

9. Certain nouns may be used as singular or as plural according to their meaning.

Acoustics (the *science*) is studied by architects.
The acoustics (*acoustic qualities*) of the hall are poor.
Athletics (*athletic training*) is part of the school program.
Athletics (*sports*) are popular with our students.
Politics (in a general sense) was behind his appointment.
Her politics (as opinions) need not concern us here.

10. Some nouns have two plurals differing in meaning.

brothers (kin)   brethren (class or society)
cloths (kinds of cloth)   clothes (wearing apparel)
indices (in mathematics)   indexes (in books)

11. Some nouns plural in form are singular in use and therefore take a singular verb.

aeronautics	economics	molasses	physics
civics	measles	news	whereabouts

12. Most compound nouns form the plural by pluralizing the fundamental part of the word.

adjutants general	trade unions
governors general	vice presidents
spelling matches	

(1) When the compound is made up of a noun and a preposition, a noun and a prepositional phrase, or a noun and an adverb, the noun is usually pluralized.

bills of lading	fillers-in	passers-by
brothers-in-law	listeners-in	runners-up
commanders in chief	lookers-on	works of art

(2) When compounds are written as one word (solid), their plurals are formed according to the usual rules for nouns.

businessmen	cupfuls	undersecretaries
bylaws	stockholders	weekends

(3) When the first element of a compound is derived from a verb, the plural is formed on the last element.

castaways	leftovers	runaways
go-betweens	letdowns	shut-ins
handouts	makeups	strikeovers

13. Nouns that retain their foreign endings form their plurals as follows: those ending in *a* change *a* to *ae*; those ending in *us* change to *i*; those ending in *um* change to *a*; those ending in *on* change to *a*; those ending in *is* change to *es*.

Many nouns retain their foreign plurals for formal and scientific material and use the English plurals in nontechnical or informal writing.

a to *ae*	alumna-alumnae (f)
	antenna-antennae-antennas (radio)
	formula-formulae-formulas
	larva-larvae-larvas
	minutia-minutiae
	vertebra-vertebrae-vertebras

us to *i*	alumnus-alumni (m)
	cactus-cacti-cactuses
	focus-foci-focuses
	fungus-fungi-funguses
	genius-genii-geniuses
	gladiolus-gladioli-gladioluses
	nucleus-nuclei-nucleuses
	radius-radii-radiuses
	stimulus-stimuli
	syllabus- syllabi-syllabuses
	terminus-termini-terminuses
um to *a*	addendum-addenda
	aquarium-aquaria-aquariums
	bacterium-bacteria
	curriculum-curricula-curriculums
	dictum-dicta-dictums
	erratum-errata
	gymnasium-gymnasia-gymnasiums
	maximum-maxima-maximums
	medium-media-mediums
	memorandum-memoranda-memorandums
	minimum-minima-minimums
	planetarium-planetaria-planetariums
	referendum-referenda-referendums
	residuum-residua-residuums
	spectrum-spectra-spectrums
	stratum-strata-stratums
	ultimatum-ultimata-ultimatums
on to *a*	automaton-automata-automatons
	criterion-criteria
	phenomenon-phenomena-phenomenons
is to *es*	analysis-analyses
	axis-axes
	basis-bases
	crisis-crises
	diagnosis-diagnoses
	ellipsis-ellipses
	emphasis-emphases
	hypothesis-hypotheses
	oasis-oases
	parenthesis-parentheses
	synopsis-synopses
	synthesis-syntheses
	thesis-theses

The following nouns also retain their foreign forms and in some cases have also an English plural:

appendix	appendices, appendixes
beau	beaux, beaus
château	châteaux, châteaus
dilettante	dilettanti, dilettantes
genus	genera
index	indices, indexes
madame	mesdames
monsieur	messieurs
tableau	tableaux, tableaus

Note that *agenda* and *data,* though plural in form, are usually considered as singular collective nouns.

14. Proper nouns form their plurals by adding *s* to the singular or *es* when the word ends in *s, z, ch, sh,* or *zh.*

(the) Carolinas	Adamses	Lynches
(two) Helens	Busches	Morrises
(the) Kennedys	Joneses	Nashes

Not: the Kennedys'; the Jones'

(1) Some proper nouns representing nationalities have the same form in the plural as in the singular.

Chinese	Japanese

(2) When titles are used with proper nouns, either the title or the proper noun may be pluralized. In informal writing or in speaking, the noun (name) is usually pluralized.

Formal	*Informal*
the Misses Barlow	the Miss Barlows
Mesdames John Penn, Henry Baxter, and William Foster (different names)	Mrs. John Penn, Mrs. Henry Baxter, and Mrs. William Foster
the Mesdames Norton (same name)	the Mrs. Nortons
Messrs. Grant and Howell	Mr. Grant and Mr. Howell

15. Plurals of letters, signs, symbols, figures, and abbreviations used as nouns are formed by adding *s* or an apostrophe and *s*. The omission of the apostrophe is gaining ground, but in some cases it must be retained for clarity, as with letters.

a's, A's	ABCs *or* ABC's	apts.
i's, I's	GIs *or* GI's	depts.
6s and 7s *or*	IOUs *or* IOU's	mfrs.
6's and 7's	IQs *or* IQ's	nos.
	M.D.s *or* M.D.'s	
	YWCAs	

Dot your i's and cross your t's.
She was a woman in her late 30s (*or* 30's).

(1) In financial contexts, the figures identifying certain securities are written without the apostrophe: *Union Pacific 2½s.*

16. Plurals of words used as nouns are formed by adding *s* if the word ends with a consonant, and an apostrophe and *s* if with a vowel sound.

ifs and buts	wherefores	do's
ins and outs	yeas and nays	oh's and ah's
ups and downs		

But: twos and threes

(1) Plurals of contractions used as nouns are formed by adding *s: do's* and *don'ts.*

Pronouns

Use of Personal Pronouns

Personal pronouns agree with their antecedents (the nouns they represent) in gender and number, but their case depends upon their construction in the clause in which they appear.

1. The nominative case (*I, you, she, he, it; we, you, they*) is used:

(1) as the subject of a verb

I shall finish the report on Tuesday.
You received a fair price for the property.
They always pay their bills promptly.

(2) as a predicate complement; that is, a pronoun following some form of the verb *to be*. (Note: the verb *to be* takes the same case after it as it takes before it.)

I think it was *they* who called.
If you were *he*, would you move to California?
Yes, it is *I*.
It was *she* who volunteered to address the circulars.

There is a tendency to use the objective case of pronouns following *to be:* it's *me*, it was *her*, it's *him*, it was *us*. This usage is acceptable in informal speaking and writing but should be avoided in formal writing.

Even in speaking, it is possible to say, "It's I" without being considered pompous. It is a question of formality and preference.

(3) in apposition with the subject of a verb

Several delegates, *he* among them, will state their opposition at the next meeting.
Most of the team, at least *we* from the upper classes, are in favor of holding extra practice sessions.

(4) as the complement of an infinitive. (When the infinitive has no subject, the pronoun following *to be* is in the nominative case to agree with the subject of the sentence.)

Greene seems to be *he* who made the protest.
The speakers are to be *they* who are running for election.

2. The objective case (*me, you, her, him, us, them*) is used:

(1) as the object of a verb

The supervisor trusted *her* to make out the payroll.
The delegates unanimously appointed *him* chairman.
Our lawyer advised *him* and *me* to sign the contract.

(2) as the indirect object of a verb

Last year the company gave *him* a bonus.
The witness told *us* the truth.

(3) in apposition with the object of a verb

The judge fined us, both *me* and my brother.
The chairman asked them all, Bent, Lowell, and *her*, to
   vote for the repeal.

(4) as subject of an infinitive

The committee invited *him* and *me* to be present. (not *he*
   and *I*)
I wish you would let *him* and *me* finish the checking. (not
   he and *I*)

(5) as object of an infinitive

The chairman asked me to invite *him* to the conference.
The buyer asked us to meet *her* at the terminal.

(6) as complement of an infinitive. (If the infinitive *to be* has a subject, that subject is in the objective case. Thus, the pronoun that follows the infinitive must be in the objective case, following the rule that the verb *to be* takes the same case after it as before it.)

The manager took *her* to be *me*.
We thought the applicants to be *them*.

(7) as the object of a preposition

No orders were received from *them* this week.
The outcome depends on *us*.

(8) when a pronoun follows *as* or *than*, it takes the form it would have if the clause were completed.

Jennifer is more competent than *I* (I am).
Charles is not so accurate as *he* (as he is).
The Blakes are better travelers than *we* (we are).

We like his brother as much as *him* (as we do him).
I trust Greene more than *him* (than I do him).

3. The possessive case (*my, mine, your, yours, his, her, hers, its, our, ours, their, theirs*) is used:

(1) to denote possession and to complete the predicate when the noun is omitted. (Note: there is no apostrophe before the *s* in the possessive of personal pronouns.)

This property is *his* (*hers*).
Is this coupon *yours* (*theirs*)?
The plan was *ours*, the details were *his*.

(2) to form a double possessive

This summary of *yours* makes the financial statement clear.
That property of *theirs* lies along the river.

(*See also* Possessive Adjectives, p. 37.)

Compound Personal Pronouns

Compound personal pronouns (*myself, yourself, himself, herself, itself, ourselves, yourselves, themselves*) are used:

4. for emphasis (intensive use)

He *himself* will pay the damages.
The secretary *herself* mailed the letter.

5. for expressing action as turned back upon the subject (reflexive use)

They will hurt *themselves* by such actions.
He convinced *himself* that the scheme would not work.

Compound personal pronouns should not be used as substitutes for personal pronouns.

The principal gave the paper to Holden and *me* (not *myself*).
Lake, Bridges, and *I* bought the building (not *myself*).

Relative Pronouns

A relative pronoun introduces a subordinate clause that modifies a noun or a pronoun occurring earlier in the sentence and connects a dependent clause to the main clause. It is also a substitute word that refers to its antecedent and stands for that antecedent in a subordinate clause.

The most frequently used relative pronouns are *who, that, which,* and *what.*

> The association elected Ellen Carr, *who* has had years of experience.
> The office *that* we wanted has been rented.
> *What* you say is correct.
> *The Careful Writer, which* you borrowed two weeks ago, is now due.

Who is the only one of the relative pronouns that changes its form to indicate case (*who, whose, whom,* as well as *whoever, whomever*). Before its case can be determined, the function it plays in a sentence must be decided.

Who, whose, and *whom* (as well as *whoever* and *whomever*) refer to persons. *That* refers to animals, persons, or things and is used to introduce restrictive clauses. *Which* refers to lower animals, things, and ideas, and introduces nonrestrictive clauses. (While *that* may refer to persons, many writers prefer to use *who* and *whom.*)

For a discussion of the distinction between restrictive and nonrestrictive clauses, *see* Clauses, p. 7.

A relative pronoun has the following functions in its own clause:

6. In the nominative case:

(1) as subject of the clause in which it stands

> The School Board interviewed all the candidates *who* applied.
> The dogs *that* appear on television are unusually well trained.
> The league will help *whoever* needs help.

Our best wishes go to Homer and Frost *who,* we are certain, have the best interests of the city at heart.

7. In the objective case:

(1) as object of a verb

We awarded the contract to the Philips Company, *which* we have dealt with in the past.
Dr. Benson is the surgeon *whom* we recommend.
I know *whomever* we ask will be criticized by some.

(2) as object of a preposition

All the men with *whom* he worked were experienced.
Maurice nominated the Rev. Gordon Major, for *whom* we all have a high regard.

(3) as subject of an infinitive

We do not know *whom* to invite as next month's speaker.
John asked *her* to play the piano.

Interrogative Pronouns

8. Interrogative pronouns (*who, which, what*) are used in asking questions. *Which* and *what* present no problems of case.

An interrogative pronoun has no antecedent in the sentence; the word to which it refers appears only in the answer.

What caused the explosion?
Whose is it?
Who addressed these envelopes?

Notice that in questions, particularly those in which the pronoun comes first and is separated from the preposition that governs it, *who* is acceptable usage.

Who was the monument named for? *But:* For *whom* was it named?
Who are you going with? *But:* With *whom* are you going?

Note: the possessive *whose* does not have an apostrophe. It should be distinguished from the contraction *who's* (*who is*).

9. The interrogatives *which, whose,* and *what* often modify nouns and are then interrogative adjectives.

Which book is due?
Whose letters are ready to be mailed?
What caller left this briefcase?

Indefinite Pronouns

Indefinite pronouns, such as *all, any, both, each, either, everybody, none, one, several, some, someone,* do not refer to specific persons or things. It should be noted, also, that many of these words may be either pronouns or adjectives, depending upon their use in the sentence.

Both of us have been assigned special work. (pronoun)
Both clerks were busy. (adjective)

Indefinite pronouns frequently present problems in number and gender. Following are suggestions for the use of these words.

10. When the indefinite pronoun is the subject of a sentence, it regularly takes a singular verb and the pronoun referring to it agrees with it in number and gender. When gender may be considered as either masculine or feminine, the masculine pronoun often is preferred, but some writers use both.

Each of you must decide for *himself.*
Neither of the candidates has expressed *his* opinion in the matter.
Every student raised *his* or *her* hand.
Has *any* of the saleswomen refused to sign *her* name to the petition?
Everybody has stated *his* views on this subject.

Note: *everyone* and *everybody* are not always referred to by a singular pronoun. The number of the pronoun following depends upon the meaning of the sentence. Modern usage accepts these words as having plural significance, and they are referred to by a plural pronoun.

Everybody comes, but *they* seldom stay through the meeting.
Everybody has considered the regulations, but *their* opinions differ.

11. As the words *both, few, many, several* are plural in meaning, they take plural verbs and are referred to by plural pronouns.

Both of the accountants sent in *their* reports.
Few cast *their* votes for Thompson.
Many of the delegates presented *their* credentials early.

12. Some indefinite pronouns, such as *all, most,* and *some,* are singular or plural depending on their meaning in a sentence.

All (everything) has been prepared for the reception.
All (the boats) have hoisted their sails.

The modern tendency is to consider *none* as plural except when it is equivalent to *no one* or *not one.* If the meaning is unmistakably singular, use *no one* or *not one.*

None have succeeded in their efforts to change the club constitution.
Not one of the partners has registered a complaint.

13. When *else* is added to a compound indefinite, the possessive is formed by adding an apostrophe and *s* (*'s*) to the word *else.*

Nobody else's decisions are more respected than yours.
Somebody else's plan may prove better than John's.

14. When compound indefinites are formed by adding *body* or *thing* to indefinite pronouns, the words thus formed are written solid: *everybody, something.* When such compounds are formed by adding *one,* they are written solid unless the reference is to each of several persons: *anyone, everyone, someone.*

Everyone listened attentively to the speaker.
Everybody arrived on time.
Can *someone* type this memorandum accurately?

Write the compounds as two words if a prepositional phrase follows:

Every one of the class attended the reunion.
Any one of the officers is willing to serve as chairman.

Verbs

A verb is a word that tells what the subject (noun, pronoun, or clause) does or what is done to it. The verb expresses action, mode of being, occurrence, or condition, and should agree with its subject in person and number.

Recognition of the Subject

1. Compound subjects.

(1) A subject consisting of two or more nouns or pronouns connected by *and* takes a plural predicate unless the nouns refer to the same person or express a single idea.

Our merchandise and equipment *are covered* by insurance.
Weather and unemployment *are cited* as causes of the decline in trade.
He and I *are* members of the Faculty Committee.
The sum and substance of the matter *is* that our firm remains in a prosperous condition. (single idea)
My friend and adviser *suggests* I take a business course. (one person)

(2) Singular subjects connected by *or* or *nor* take a singular verb.

Either the secretary or the treasurer *is* always present at every meeting.
Neither Black nor Nichols *fears* the court's decision.

(3) When two subjects differing in number are connected by *either-or* or *neither-nor* and one of the

subjects is plural, it should be placed second and the verb should agree with it in number.

> Correct: Neither the *candidate* nor the *voters are satisfied* with the proposal.
> Incorrect: Neither the voters nor the candidate is satisfied with the proposal.
> Incorrect: Neither the voters nor the candidate are satisfied with the proposal.

2. A verb should agree with its subject, not with a noun placed between the verb and its subject.

> This *list* of addresses *was* prepared by Horton.
> The latest *news* about those accidents *has* just been received.
> The *report* about conditions in the slum areas *was* published last week.

3. Phrases or clauses introduced by such expressions as *together with, as well as, in addition to* are not part of the subject and, therefore, do not affect the number of the verb.

> The *church*, as well as the nearby stores, *was* destroyed by fire.
> The *problem* of building more schools, in addition to paying teachers' salaries for them, *was* discussed by the board.
> All *indications*, as far as we can see, *point* to better business.

4. When the verb precedes the subject, care should be taken to have it agree with its subject in number.

> In this catalog *are* the *requirements* for admission, the courses, and the fees.
> Howe stated that there *were reports* on the budget to be considered at the April meeting.

5. The form of plural nouns, especially those ending in *a*, which require a plural verb, should not be mistaken for the singular form: *bacteria, criteria, phenomena.* (*See* pp. 11–12.)

6. With fractions, the verb agrees with the noun in the prepositional phrase.

Half of the *road was* blocked off.
Half of the roads were blocked off.
One third of the *tax goes* to the county.
One third of the *taxes go* to the county.

7. When nouns of quantity, distance, time, and amount are thought of as a unit, the verb should be singular.

Forty pounds *is* enough for the present.
Twenty dollars *is* still *due* on John's account.
Four years *is* usually *required* for a B.A. degree.
Two hundred miles *remains* to be driven in the morning.

8. Subjects modified by *each* and *every* are singular and therefore require a singular verb.

Each boy gets an apple.
Every street in the town is well lighted.

9. Collective nouns as subjects.
   A collective noun is a noun that names a group of persons, animals, or things: *committee, herd, furniture.*
   Such nouns may be regarded as singular or plural: singular, if the word denotes a group acting as an individual; plural, if the word denotes the individuals that make up the group.

The jury *has* (not *have*) agreed upon the verdict.
The jury *have* (not *has*) disagreed as to their verdict.
The Community Service Committee *were* (not *was*) divided on *their* (not *its*) understanding of the question.
When your committee *has* (not *have*) completed *its* (not *their*) work *it* (not *they*) should prepare a report.

(1) Since the names of associations, boards, companies, corporations, and the like are collective nouns, they should be regarded as singular if the name denotes a group acting as an individual or as an entity and plural if the name denotes the individuals composing the group. Care must be taken to have the pronouns and the verbs agree with the collective nouns.

The American Association of University Women *has* urged *its* members to contribute to the Scholarship Fund.
The Southeastern Coast Line *is* agreeable to your suggestion. . . . *It* has adopted a progressive public relations program and *is* receiving encouraging support.
The Hall Company *has* scheduled the largest promotional program *it* has ever placed behind any of *its* more than 1,000 products.

Some authorities regard a company name with a plural ending or makeup as plural; as, *Haines Brothers, Upjohn Publishers, L. M. Gordon and Sons.* Most firms with such endings, however, regard their titles as singular. This is true, for instance, of *Charles Scribner's Sons* and of *Brooks Brothers.*

Because the use of *it* or *its* to refer to an association, a company, a corporation, or any other entity may seem unsuitable or stilted, the plural pronouns, *they, their, them* may sometimes be preferred. Then, of course, the verb must also be plural.

As the copyright of the book is held by The Macmillan Company, you must have *their* permission to reproduce this extract. If you ask *them, they* are not likely to refuse you.

(2) The article *a* usually precedes a collective noun regarded as plural; the article *the* usually precedes a collective noun regarded as singular.

A number of students have signified their intention to take the advanced course.
The number of students in economics has increased this year.
A majority of voters are opposed to the amendment.
The majority in an assembly has the right to decide what the action shall be.
A couple of suggestions were offered by the audience.
The couple was recognized boarding a plane.

Voice of Verbs

The voice of a verb shows whether the subject of the verb has performed the action (active voice) or has received the action (passive voice).

> Active voice: Bill *has washed* his car.
> Passive voice: The car *is washed* every week.

The subject of the verb (*see* pp. 22–25) may be a noun or pronoun, a phrase, or an entire clause. In all cases, it will provide the answer to *who* or *what*.

> *Who* washed the car?   *What* was washed?

The verb in the passive voice consists of a form of *to be* combined with the past participle of the main verb:

I was eating when I *was called* to the telephone.
You *have been waited on* all your life.
The need for better housing *was discussed* at the workshop.
Everything you could wish for *was given* to you as a child.
This book *will be used* in adult education classes.
The house *was being* painted.

Transitive and Intransitive Verbs

Transitive verbs show action, either upon someone or something. A verb in the active voice shows that an action has passed over to the receiver or object.

> The Winterthur Museum *sells* reproductions of its treasures.
> Who knows what next year *will bring?*
> We each *do* our own laundry.

When action is passed back to the subject, the verb is passive.

> Reproductions *are sold* at the Winterthur Museum.
> Personal laundry *is done* by each resident.
> An action *has been brought* against the owner of the truck.

In another situation, the subject receives the results of the action, again in the passive voice.

The baby *was given* a football by his proud father.
Lyndon Johnson *was sworn* in as President after John Kennedy's assassination.
Our guests *are offered* complimentary drinks on their arrival.

Some verbs of action have no receiver and are intransitive.

The children *played* in the backyard.
The wind *whistled* among the bare branches of the trees.
Tomorrow we *can sleep* late.

When an action is indicated, the same verb becomes transitive.

My nephew *plays* football at Michigan State.
Peter *whistles* a tune while he cooks breakfast.
Tonight you *can sleep* the sleep of the just.

Included with intransitive verbs are the *linking verbs: appear, be, become, feel, grow, keep, look, remain, seem, smell, sound, stay,* and *taste.* These verbs link the subject to a noun or pronoun (called the predicate nominative) or to an adjective (the predicate adjective).

The predicate nominative provides another name for the subject:

Henry became a grandfather this year.
The general was emperor for life.

The predicate adjective describes the subject:

All your plants look healthy.
This room smells smoky.
The entire dinner was perfectly delicious.

Tense

Tense is a distinctive form of a verb that expresses the time of action. Tense is indicated by inflection, that is, a change in the form of the verb itself (sing, sang, look, looked) or by the use of auxiliary verb forms (*will* sing; *have* looked).

Present:

10. The *present* tense indicates that an action is going on at the present time.

This sale *offers* unusually low prices on all furniture.
I *am* glad to accept your invitation.

11. The *present* tense is used to express a present fact or an unchangeable truth.

The Rocky Mountains *are* the longest and highest mountain system in North America.
The teacher explained that water *is* composed of two gases.

12. The *present* tense may indicate customary action.

The Committee *meets* on the first Thursday of every month.

13. The *present* tense is often used instead of the future tense, although the latter would be more precise. This usage is considered by some authorities to be colloquial, for speaking or informal writing.

College *opens* next month.
We *leave* for London in June.

14. The *present* tense is sometimes used to make a past event or a past statement more graphic; this usage is called the historical present.

Dickens *is* at his best in depicting the tragedies of childhood.
Emerson *says*, "To be great is to be misunderstood."
The Declaration of Independence *states* that all men are created equal.

15. The *present* tense should *not* be used to express an action begun in the past and still continuing; the correct tense is the *present perfect*.

I *have lived* (*not* am living) in Boston for ten years.
I *have known* (*not* know) this man all my life.

Past:

16. The *past* tense indicates an action that occurred in past time.

I *answered* Frost's letter yesterday.
The commission *filed* its report several days ago.

17. The *present perfect* tense denotes an action that has been completed at some indefinite time before the present time.

The mayor *has spent* many hours on the budget.
We *have given* the merger careful consideration.

18. The *past perfect* tense denotes that the action of the verb was completed at some definite point in past time.

Before I worked for Horton & Chase, I *had* never *seen* a computer.
If he *had remained* with us, he would have been promoted.

Note the correct use of tenses in the following sentences:

He didn't find the book.
He hasn't found the book yet.
He hadn't found the book when the librarian asked for it.
I have visited most of the capitals of Europe.
I have been ten years in America.
He always has paid and always will pay his bills.
Not: He always has and always will pay his bills.

Future: Shall and Will

Until recent years, the best American usage preferred *shall* for the first person, to indicate simply futurity, willingness, and expectation.

I *shall send* my check tomorrow.
We *shall do* as you suggest.
As far as I know, I *shall attend* the Little Rock meeting.

Will was used for the second and third persons, to indicate the same simple futurity, willingness, and expectation.

The plane *will leave* at noon.
You *will find* the hotel comfortable.
He *will come* as soon as he can.
They *will know* where to find us.

However, most writers today use *will* for all three persons to show futurity, as well as determination, promise, and willingness. To emphasize intent, such adverbs as *certainly, surely,* and the like can be added.

We will certainly do our best to locate a suitable substitute.
He will surely be able to complete the repairs on time.

But: in questions and requests it seems more natural to use *shall* in the first person and *will* in the second and third persons.

Shall I call for you at nine o'clock?
How long *shall* we hold your reservation?
Will the person who took my coat by mistake please return it.
Will you please have this report on my desk by Thursday morning.

Future: Should and Would

The use of *should* and *would,* the past tenses of *shall* and *will,* is no longer so strictly observed as formerly. However, conventional usage advocates the following rules:

19. Use *should* in all persons to denote an obligation, in the sense of "ought to."

We *should* settle this problem at once.
You *should* pay the damage to the other driver's car.
The board *should* agree on the proposed bylaws.

20. Use *would* in all persons to denote habitual action or a wish.

I *would* never send out letters with erasures.
Blake *would* always report as soon as he finished the job.
Once a week the heads of departments *would* meet to discuss policies.
I wish that you *would* accept the chairmanship.

21. Use *should* in a conditional clause introduced by *if* to express contingency or simple futurity.

If I *should* decide to go, I will call you Thursday.
If he *should* accept the nomination, he will undoubtedly be appointed.

Tense of the Infinitive:

22. The infinitive has two tenses, present and present perfect. Which tense to use depends upon the time expressed by the main verb.

(1) The present infinitive denotes the same time or future time in relation to the action of the main verb. Notice that in the following sentences the present infinitive is used with verbs denoting present or past time. The time denoted by the infinitive is the same as that of the principal verb or later than denoted by the principal verb.

I intend *to go* tomorrow.
I intended *to go* Thursday.
For several days I have been intending *to write* to you.
I should have liked *to do* it, but I could not (not *to have done it*).
Jim would have liked *to go* with his brother last week (not *to have gone*).
I had intended *to write* the letter before breakfast (not *to have written*).

(2) The perfect infinitive denotes action that is complete at the time of the principal verb.

The submarine was reported *to have been sighted* off Bermuda at noon.

(3) Note the difference in meaning implied by the present and perfect infinitives in the following sentences:

His men believed Washington *to be* a great general.
We believe Washington *to have been* a great general.
The Milan Cathedral is said *to be* one of the largest in the world.
The Parthenon is said *to have been* erected in the Age of Pericles.

The Subjunctive Mood

23. The subjunctive mood is little used today except in a few special cases:

(1) To express a wish.

I wish I *were* in Europe.

(2) To express a contrary-to-fact condition.

If I *were* you, I should take the position.

(3) Present and past conditions may be either (A) noncommittal or (B) contrary to fact.

A. A condition is noncommittal when it implies nothing as to the truth or falsity of the case supposed.

If James is angry, I am sorry. (Perhaps James is angry, perhaps not.)

B. A condition is contrary to fact when it implies that the supposed case is not or was not true.

If James were angry, I should be sorry. (James is *not* angry.)

In a noncommittal present condition, the *if* clause takes the present indicative; in a noncommittal past condition, the past, the perfect, or the pluperfect.

The conclusion may be in any form that the sense allows.

Present condition, noncommittal:

If this pebble is a diamond, it is valuable.

Past condition, noncommittal:

If that pebble was a diamond, it was valuable.
If Tom has apologized, he has done his duty.
If John had reached home before we started, he must have made a quick journey.

In each of these examples, the speaker declines to commit himself as to the truth of the supposed case. Perhaps the pebble was a diamond, perhaps not;

Tom may or may not have apologized; whether or not John had reached home, we cannot tell.

Principal Parts

24. The principal parts of verbs consist of the present and the past indicative, and the past or perfect participle.

The following table shows the principal parts of many troublesome verbs, most of which are irregular. Illiterate and careless errors occur most often in the use of the past tense and the past participle; as, *has went* for *has gone*, *sunk* for *sank*.

Present	*Past*	*Past Participle*
am or be	was	been
arise	arose	arisen
awake	awoke	awaked
bear	bore	borne
beat	beat	beaten
begin	began	begun
bend	bent	bent
beseech	besought	besought
bid (card playing)	bid	bid
bid (most senses)	bade, bid	bidden, bid
bleed	bled	bled
blow	blew	blown
break	broke	broken
bring	brought	brought
broadcast	broadcast	broadcast
catch	caught	caught
choose	chose	chosen
climb	climbed	climbed
cling	clung	clung
come	came	come
dive	dived	dived
do	did	done
draw	drew	drawn
drink	drank	drunk
drive	drove	driven
fall	fell	fallen
fight	fought	fought

flee	fled	fled
flow	flowed	flowed
fly	flew	flown
forbid	forbade	forbidden
forget	forgot	forgotten
forsake	forsook	forsaken
freeze	froze	frozen
get	got	got, gotten
go	went	gone
grow	grew	grown
hang (most senses)	hung	hung
hang (punishment)	hanged	hanged
hide	hid	hidden
hurt	hurt	hurt
kneel	knelt, kneeled	knelt, kneeled
lay (to put; to place)	laid	laid
lead	led	led
leap	leaped, leapt	leaped, leapt
lie (to recline)	lay	lain
lie (to tell a falsehood)	lied	lied
loose	loosed	loosed
lose	lost	lost
pay	paid	paid
plead	pleaded	pleaded
prove	proved	proved, proven
ring	rang, rung	rung
rise	rose	risen
run	ran	run
say	said	said
see	saw	seen
seek	sought	sought
set (to place)	set	set
shake	shook	shaken
shine	shone	shone
show	showed	shown, showed
shrink	shrank, shrunk	shrunk
sing	sang, sung	sung
sink	sank	sunk
sit (to sit down)	sat	sat
slay	slew	slain
sleep	slept	slept
speak	spoke	spoken
stay	stayed	stayed
steal	stole	stolen

stick	stuck	stuck
sting	stung	stung
stop	stopped	stopped
strive	strove	striven
swear	swore	sworn
swim	swam	swum
swing	swung	swung
take	took	taken
teach	taught	taught
tear	tore	torn
throw	threw	thrown
tread	trod	trodden, trod
wake	waked, woke	waked
wear	wore	worn
weave	wove	woven
win	won	won
wring	wrung	wrung
write	wrote	written

Adjectives and Adverbs

An adjective is a word used to modify (limit, identify, or describe) a noun. An adverb is a word used to modify the meaning of a verb, an adjective, or another adverb.

1. An adjective is used when the condition of the subject is described.

   The discussion was *brief.*
   A *reasonable* decision should be expected soon.

2. An adverb is used when the action of the verb is explained.

   He always speaks *clearly* over the telephone.
   The mayor answered the complaint *quietly* and *reasonably.*

3. Some words have the same form whether they are used as adjectives or adverbs: *far, fast, first.*

   The little inn was a *far* cry from our usual accommodations.
   Holt ran *far* ahead of the other contestants.
   He liked to drive *fast* sportscars.
   He typed so *fast* he made many mistakes.

The *first* candidate spoke at length.
First, watch your spelling.

4. Some words have two adverbial forms: *cheap, cheaply; direct, directly; loud, loudly; quick, quickly; slow, slowly; sure, surely; wide, widely.* The choice is a matter of usage with *ly* forms ordinarily considered more formal, the shorter forms more emphatic. The adjective is used whenever some form of the verb *to be* or *to seem* may be substituted. But when no such substitution can be made, the adverb is generally preferred.

> Buy *cheap* and sell dear.
> The dresses were *cheaply* made.
> Mail the order *direct* to me.
> The clerk went *directly* home.
> Don't speak so *loud.*
> The child called *loudly* to the lifeguard.
> Go *slow.*
> Burns drove so *slowly* that he was late.

5. The modifier should be an adjective if it denotes the condition of the subject, but an adverb if it explains the action of the verb.

> We stand *firm* in our opinion.
> We stand *firmly* by our decision.
> They stood *silent* as the ambulance passed.
> They listened *silently* to the soloist.
> The house has been restored *complete* in every detail.
> The house has been *completely* restored.
> The patient remained *quiet.*
> He walked *quietly* around the room.

6. Verbs of the senses, such as *feel, look, smell, sound,* and *taste,* as well as copulative verbs, such as *appear, be, become, seem,* take an adjective to denote the quality or the condition of the subject.

> Everybody *feels* happy about John's appointment.
> Fowler always *looks* cheerful.
> The flowers *smell* sweet.
> All the food *tasted* delicious.

The new secretary *appears* competent.
The patient *seems* better today.
George felt *bad* (*or* felt *badly*) about the delay.

Bad and *badly* are found with almost equal acceptance in standard English when following *feel*, although *bad* is usually preferred in formal writing. . . . When preceded by *look, sound, smell,* etc., the usual choice is *bad.*

The Random House Dictionary

7. Possessive Adjectives

The forms *my, our, your,* and *their* are possessive adjectives, as are also *his, her,* and *its,* when used to modify nouns.

His property is now worthless.
Their plans included a trip to Europe.

Possessive adjectives also modify gerunds (verb forms ending in *ing* used as nouns).

His leaving the company came as a surprise to us.
We could not think of *his* refusing our offer.
Is there any possibility of *their* buying a house in Cambridge?

Comparison

8. The comparative degree is used in comparing two persons or things. The superlative degree is used in comparing more than two persons or things.

Our expenses are *greater* than yours.
This route is *more direct* than the one through town.
Baxter & Grant's material is *less expensive* than yours.
You are the *best* swimmer on the team.

9. Adjectives of one syllable and some adjectives of two syllables form the comparative by adding *er,* and the superlative by adding *est,* to the positive.

fine	finer	finest
friendly	friendlier	friendliest

Many adjectives of two syllables and most adjectives of more than two syllables form their comparative by prefixing *more* or *less,* and their superlative by prefixing *most* or *least.*

The recent news of the expedition seemed *more hopeful.*
As a businessman he became *most successful.*
Long is the *least competent* salesman in the department.

10. Some adjectives have irregular comparative and superlative forms. If in doubt about the forms, consult a dictionary.

bad, ill	worse	worst
far	farther (distance)	farthest
	further (in the sense of additional, and also distance)	furthest
good, well	better	best
little	less, lesser	least
	littler	littlest
much, many	more	most

11. Strictly, some adjectives and the adverbs derived from them are incapable of comparison because they express a quality complete or perfect; as, *universal, unique, perfect, infinite, preferable.* But modern usage accepts many deviations from this rule; a *most complete* report, a *more perfect* example.

Such words, however, may be modified in meaning by such adverbs as *almost, hardly, nearly,* to suggest approach to the superlative.

The Articles

12. Use the indefinite article *a* before words in which the first sound is a consonant, a sounded *h,* or a long *u.*

a cabinet	a hundred pounds
a helper	a unanimous vote
a heroic rescue	a united nation
a historical novel	a union
a history	a useful machine
a hotel	

13. Use *an* before words in which the first sound is a vowel, except long *u*, and before words beginning with silent *h*.

an envelope	an hour
an owner	an unnecessary word

14. The articles *a, an,* and *the* should be repeated in referring to two separate persons or objects.

The company employs *a* typist and *a* stenographer. (two persons)
The company employs *a* typist and stenographer. (one person)
Either *a* man or *a* woman may apply.
For sale: *a* maple and *a* mahogany desk. (two desks)
For sale: *a* maple and mahogany desk. (one desk)

But when two or more nouns refer to the same person, the article should not be repeated.

Caesar was *a* general, writer, and statesman.
Martin became well known as *a* poet and novelist.

Proper Adjectives

15. A proper adjective is a descriptive adjective derived from a proper noun: *American* industry, *French* literature, *Mexican* silver.

(1) Capitalize proper adjectives unless they have lost their association with the nouns from which they were derived: *chili* sauce, *french* fry, *panama* hat, *pasteurized* milk, *platonic* love, *turkish* towels. (*See also* p. 73.)

Agreement of Adjective and Noun

16. *This* and *that* are singular and must be used to modify singular nouns. *These* and *those* are plural and must be used to modify plural nouns.

This kind (not *these* kind) of books is instructive.
These kinds (not *these* kind) of books are instructive.
That sort (not *those* sort) of answer carries little weight.

Note: I feel *kind of* sorry for him is incorrect. Say *rather* sorry.

Note that *kind of* (not *kind of a*) and *sort of* (not *sort of a*) are permissible although colloquial.

That *kind of* (not *kind of a*) boy ranks high.
That *sort of* (not *sort of a*) position is what I want.

Placement of Adverbs

17. The position of an adverb affects the meaning of the sentence.

The bookkeeper made *only* one error. (*not:* only made)
He *only* nominated Jones for president. (He did not vote for him.)
He nominated *only* Jones for president. (He did not nominate anyone else.)

18. An adverb should usually be placed as near as possible to the word it modifies.

It seems *almost impossible* to finish the manuscript by June. (*not:* almost seems)
Do you remember *ever signing* such an order? (*not:* ever remember)

19. An adverb should be placed first in a sentence when it is meant to qualify the whole sentence or when it is used emphatically.

Fortunately no one was in the shop when the fire broke out.
Greatly to his surprise, he was voted chairman.

20. With a compound verb, the adverb is usually placed between the parts of the compound verb.

The customer will *undoubtedly* find our statement correct.
You are *probably* right.

21. Place the adverb before the participle when it modifies the participle only.

For years the company has been *competently* managed.

Unnecessary Adverbs

22. Unnecessary adverbs should be avoided.

Each sheet of paper should be carefully numbered (not numbered *throughout*).
Repeat it (not repeat it *again*).
They returned (not returned *back*) to the hotel.
Let us cooperate (not cooperate *together*).
Finish the business (not finish *up* the business).
They expect to divide (not divide *up*) the proceeds.

For the correct use of special adjectives and adverbs, *see* page 38.

Prepositions

1. A preposition is a connecting word that shows the relation of a noun or a pronoun to some other word in a sentence.

The main office is *in* Boston.

The preposition *in* shows the relation of the noun *Boston* to the verb *is*.

2. Care must be taken in the use of prepositions. A dictionary should always be consulted in case of doubt as to correct usage. The following illustrations may be helpful:

among, between
(Use *among* with more than two; *between* with two.)

The candy was divided *among* (not *between*) the members of the class.
The candy was divided *between* (not *among*) the two children.

at, with
(*with* a person, *at* a thing)

Jane was angry *with* (not *at*) me.
The minority was angry *at* (not *with*) the passage of the resolution.

The lawyer was displeased *with* (not *at*) the witness.

beside, besides
(at the side of, in addition to)

George walked *beside* (not *besides*) Mary.
Besides (not *beside*) the large doors, there are several smaller ones.

back of, behind

They ran *behind* (not *back of* or *in back of*) the garage.

in, into

The boy walked *in* the room (within its walls).
The boy walked *into* (entered) the room.

of

The phrases *could of, must of,* are erroneous forms for *could have, must have.*

Idiomatic Prepositional Phrases

adapted for	The apartment is adapted for housekeeping.
adapted to	Helen soon adapted herself to her changed circumstances.
adapted from	The story is adapted from the French.
agree on	The faculty agreed on limiting the number of students.
agree to	Do you agree to this proposition?
agree with	He agrees with me on the matter.
argue about	Do not argue about the question.
argue for	They argued for the abolition of child labor.
argue with	He argued with me about prohibition.
confide in	May I confide in you?
confide to	She confided her troubles to me.
consist in	Success does not always consist in achieving wealth.
consist of	The play consists of five acts.

denounce as	Arnold was denounced as a traitor.
denounce for	The thief was denounced for his crime.
die from	They died from exposure.
die of	She died of pneumonia.
differ about	We differ about the success of coeducation.
differ from	Mary differs from her sister in appearance.
differ in	Mother and Father differ in their opinions about our summer vacation.
differ on	They usually differ on religious questions.
differ with	I differ with you in regard to the discipline of the school.
disappointed by	We are disappointed by her mother, who failed to come.
disappointed in	Farmers are often disappointed in their yearly income.
disappointed with	The owners are disappointed with the poor prospects for sale of the property.
enter at	Enter at the front gate. He entered his son at Harvard.
enter for	John has entered for the championship.
enter in	He has entered the bill in his accounts.
enter into	The faculty entered into an agreement with the townspeople.
enter upon	He entered upon his new work with enthusiasm.
impatient at	The superintendent was impatient at the delay.
impatient with	Mother was impatient with the boys.
live at	He lives at the Hotel Astor.
live in	Helen lives in Florida.
live on	He lives on Magnolia Avenue.
prejudice against	No one is prejudiced against you.
reconcile to	He was reconciled to his father.
reconcile with	These opinions can be reconciled with hers.

Necessary Prepositions

3. Prepositions should not be omitted when they are needed to make the meaning clear. In the following sentences note the need for the italicized prepositions:

It is *of* no use to object.
Barbara will be *at* home tomorrow.
The tree was a foot *in* diameter.
Will you refrain *from* reading aloud?
His remark is unworthy *of* your notice.
They are going either to France or *to* Italy.
On this side of the river is a group of houses.
An appointment with the dentist prevented Rose *from* going to the concert.
You will find reading a comfort in youth as well as *in* later life.
The states of the East and *of* the West stood together on the question.
I had no faith *in*, or hope *for*, the movement.

Unnecessary Prepositions

4. Prepositions should be omitted when they are not needed to make the meaning clear. In the following illustrations note the unnecessary prepositions:

The girls in the school were all *about* (not *of about*) sixteen.
No one can help observing (not *from* observing) her.
Let us examine (not examine *into*) the room.
The class entered (not entered *into*) the room.
They are going home (not *to* home).
The tree is *near* (not *near to*) the garage.
The child fell *off* (not *off of*) the chair.
They sail *about* (not *on about*) the thirteenth of June.
The club disbanded *about* (not *at about*) ten.
Where has John been (not *been at*)?
Where shall we go (not *go to*)?
She does not remember (not *remember of*) any such happening.

Conjunctions

1. Conjunctions are used to connect words, phrases, or clauses. The correct use of conjunctions can be confusing. Note the following examples of good usage:

as, as if

Do *as* (not *like*) the manager suggests.
I feel *as if* (not *like*) I need a change.

that

He doesn't see *that* (not *as*) he ought to do it.
The reason for his absence was *that* (not *because*) he felt ill.
I saw in the paper *that* (not *where*) Bankhurst became president.
He told them *that* (not *how*) he expected to go to South America.

whether

I don't know *whether* (not *as*) I can go.
I shall ask him *whether* (not *if*) he will do the work.
She didn't say *whether* (not *if*) she has seen the exhibit.

Correlative Conjunctions

2. Correlative conjunctions, that is, conjunctions used in pairs, should be placed next to the words they connect. These words or expressions should be in parallel construction.

The most common correlatives are *either–or, neither–nor, not only–but also, both–and, whereas–therefore, whether–or.*

They have read neither the book nor the magazine.
Not: They have neither read the book nor the magazine.
The work gave me both pleasure and experience.
Not: The work both gave me pleasure and experience.
We visited not only London, but also Paris, Nice, and Rome.
Not: We not only visited London, but also Paris, Nice, and Rome.

With coordinate conjunctions such as *and* and *but*, ideas must be expressed in similar construction.

He was strong in body and in mind.
Or: He was strong physically and mentally.
Not: He was strong in body and also mentally.

Subordinate Conjunctions

3. When one idea in a sentence is dependent upon another, a subordinate conjunction is used to connect the dependent with the main thought. Choose the appropriate conjunction to show the relationship between the clauses.

To show cause:	*as, because, inasmuch as, now that, since*
To indicate concession:	*although, even if, though*
To express a condition:	*but that, except that, if, if only, in case, provided that, unless*
To make a comparison:	*as, as if, more than, rather than, than*
To show manner:	*as, as if*
To explain place:	*where, wherever*
To indicate purpose:	*in order that, so that, that*
To express result:	*so that, so . . . as, so . . . that, such . . . that*
To fix a time:	*after, as, as long as, as often as, before, ever since, just as, now that, since, till, until, when, whenever, whereupon, while*

Subordinate Clauses

1. Avoid interlocking subordinate clauses. Rephrasing the sentence, even dividing a long sentence into two, will be an improvement.

Poor: The price the manager quoted me was lower than I had expected, although I had heard that the real estate market was somewhat weaker than last year.
Better: The price the manager quoted me was lower than I had expected. However, I had heard that the real estate market was somewhat weaker than last year.
Poor: When I asked for reservations, I was told the hotel would be unable to accommodate us at the time we wished

to come but that we might be able to find a nearby hotel with available rooms at the price we wanted to pay.

Better: When I asked for reservations, I was told the hotel would be unable to accommodate us at the time we wished to come. The clerk did say that we might be able to find a nearby hotel with available rooms at the price we wanted to pay.

2. Subordinate clauses should be placed near the words they modify. Misplaced clauses can result in confusing or absurd statements.

Poor: The car was parked in the driveway when I arrived and appeared to have been struck from behind.

Better: When I arrived, the car was parked in the driveway and appeared to have been struck from behind.

Poor: The police have arrested the man identified by the father of the victim who saw him leaving the scene of the crime.

Better: The police have arrested a man identified by the victim's father as the man he saw leaving the scene of the crime.

Poor: While a bugler played "To the Colors," the first flag was hoisted on Grimm Park's 40-foot flagpole, followed by Martha Ferris singing the national anthem.

Better: While a bugler played "To the Colors," the first flag was hoisted on Grimm Park's 40-foot flagpole. Martha Ferris then sang the national anthem.

CHAPTER FOUR

Capitalization

1. Capitalize the first word of every sentence, whether or not it is a complete sentence.

A secretary's greatest asset is good judgment. No doubt about it.

2. Capitalize the first word of every line of poetry.

> To the glory that was Greece,
> And the grandeur that was Rome.
>
> EDGAR ALLAN POE

In some modern English poetry forms, only the first word of the first line is capitalized, and sometimes even this is written lower-case.

> Yes, light is speech. Free frank
> impartial sunlight, moonlight,
> starlight, lighthouse light,
> are language.
>
> MARIANNE MOORE

3. Capitalize all proper nouns that are names of individuals.

Mary Louise DuGarm   J. Allan McIlvaine

(1) Capitalize epithets added to proper names or applied to people or places.

the Miami Dolphins	the Empire State
William the Conqueror	the Golden Gate
Old Blue Eyes	the Windy City
the Great Communicator	the Sun Belt

(2) Capitalize *father* and *mother* when used in address, but do not capitalize such nouns when a possessive pronoun is used with them.

Yes, Mother, I am going.
My father is at home.

(3) Capitalize *uncle, aunt,* and other family terms when used with a proper noun.

I heard Aunt Lucille say that my uncle was out of town.

4. Capitalize prefixes in the names of persons as follows:

(1) In foreign names such prefixes as *d', da, della, van,* and *von* are capitalized unless preceded by a given name or title.

D'Amato; Louis d'Amato
De Paul; Cardinal de Paul
Van Kirk; A. B. van Kirk

(2) In American and British names such prefixes are usually capitalized even if preceded by a given name or title, but it is best to determine individual preference if possible.

Justice Van Dusen   Henry van Dyke
Oliver de Water   R. J. DiLeo
Laura von Schmidt   Maria De Santis

Note also that a space may or may not be left between the prefix and the rest of the name, depending on individual preference.

References for authoritative capitalization of American and British names: *Who's Who, Who's Who in America, Dictionary of National Biography, Dictionary of American Biography.*

5. Capitalize all academic degrees following the name whether abbreviated or written out.

Allan G. Buchmann, Litt.D.; Jean Davies, Ph.D.; George Schuster, J.D.; Patricia Atwater, LL.D.; Marion Holtz, Master of Arts.

(1) When writing more than one degree after a name, arrange according to their importance, the most important last; when they are of the same rank, as various doctoral degrees, according to the time of their being granted. (*See* p. 118.)

Arthur J. Brookins, LL.B., M.A.
George D. Coleman, Ph.D., Litt.D., LL.D.
Saul R. Grossman, M.D., Ph.D.

6. Capitalize all academic and religious titles; as, *Doctor, Bishop, Professor, Dean,* when preceding a name.

Dr. Donald Lawlor, Bishop McAleer, Professor Louis Lowenstein, Dean Barbara Black.

(1) With *Reverend,* other academic titles and abbreviations for academic degrees may be used. The following are correct forms for the use of *Reverend:*

Rev. John Blake	minister, pastor, rector, or Roman Catholic
The Reverend John Blake	priest, without doctoral degrees

The Reverend John Blake, D.D.
The Reverend Dr. John Blake
The Reverend President John Blake
The Reverend Professor John Blake
The Very Reverend Dean John Blake
The Right Reverend John Blake (Bishop)
The Most Reverend John Blake (Archbishop)
The Very Reverend John Blake (Monsignor)
The Reverend Mother Superior

The article *the* when preceding *Reverend* in a sentence should not be capitalized. The abbreviation *Rev.* should not be used when preceded by *the*.

On Sunday *the* (not *The*) Reverend Roy Gates will preside. We heard *the Reverend* (not *The Rev.*) Roy Gates.

(2) The title *Reverend* is an adjective, not a noun, and must, therefore, always be used with a given

name or initials on the envelope or in writing the inside address; as,

Rev. John L. Blake   *or*   Rev. J. L. Blake
not
Rev. Blake

It is permissible, however, in referring to a clergyman in the body of a letter, to write

Rev. Mr. Blake   *or*   Rev. Dr. Blake

although it is considered better form to use the given name with the title in even such a reference.

(3) The titles *Reverend* and *Doctor* are usually abbreviated, but are often spelled out in formal use. *Reverend* is not used in the salutation of a letter. Where there is no other title, the salutation is *Dear Mr. _____, Dear Mrs. _____, or Dear Miss _____.*

(4) Do not capitalize the following when they stand alone (*see* Rule 9):

judge	cantor	rabbi
justice	elder	rector
principal	minister (of religion)	attaché
professor	pastor	consul
superintendent	priest	consul general

The rector has engaged a new secretary.
Did the professor receive his class list from the registrar or from the clerk?
The judge asked the assistant director for all data on the case.

7. Capitalize all titles of rank, honor, or respect when preceding the name.

President _____	Speaker _____
Vice President _____	Governor _____
the Earl of _____	Mayor _____
General _____	Cardinal _____
Senator _____	Chief Justice _____
Congressman _____	Under Secretary _____

Note: *GPO Style Manual* states, "In official usage, the title Vice President of the United States is written without a hyphen." In general usage, this title may also be written in two words.

8. Capitalize all Government titles when referring to definite persons in high positions or to their positions, and all titles of honor or nobility when referring to specific persons.

the Secretary of Defense
the Secretary of the
  Treasury
the Assistant Secretary of
  the Treasury
Acting Secretary of State
Associate Justice of the
  Supreme Court
Chairman of the
  Committee of the Whole
the Speaker of the House
the Congressman from
  Maine

the Senator from Florida
House Chaplain
Director, U.S. Coast and
  Geodetic Survey
the Queen of England
the President of the French
  Republic
the Archbishop of
  Canterbury
the Governor General of
  Canada
the Duke of Norfolk

9. Capitalize a title of preeminence or distinction following the name of a person or when used alone as a substitute for the name.

Ronald W. Reagan, fortieth President of the United States; the President; the Chief Executive; the Commander in Chief
John Smith, Secretary of Agriculture; the Secretary
James Blank, Governor of Arkansas; the Governor of Arkansas; the Governor
Stephen Jones, President-elect

(1) Titles of city, county, or state officials (except Governor) are usually not capitalized except as a form of courtesy in the body of a letter, in the inside address, and after the signature.

Robert Frank, mayor of Exville
George Howell, city clerk
Lawrence Bradshaw, county treasurer
Horace Franklin, state superintendent of schools

(2) In reports and in correspondence, business titles referring to positions of authority are usually capitalized as a form of courtesy when they refer to definite individuals or when a company refers to its own officers.

> Lewis Barr, President of the Southern Cotton Association, called the meeting to order.
> The Chairman of the Board of Arnold & Cole was authorized by the stockholders to increase the dividend.

(3) In material for publication in newspapers, magazines, or books, the title following a name is usually not capitalized.

> Dr. John D. Smith, provost of the College of Agriculture
> G. E. Schuster, chairman of the Public Utility Council

10. Titles are sometimes used instead of the names of those who bear them. In such cases, when a definite person is referred to in the singular number, the title is to be capitalized.

(1) In the second person if used as synonyms of proper names.

> Mr. Secretary, please examine the report.
> You will report, Captain, to Headquarters.
> Do you think, Senator, this bill will pass?

Do not capitalize *sir, madam, monsieur,* and such terms used alone in address.

> What plan would you suggest, sir?
> Why, madam, look what it means.

> And so, my fellow citizens, the reason that I came away from Washington is that I sometimes get lonely down there.
>
> WOODROW WILSON

(2) In the third person.

> When the Governor, escorted by local Democrats, appeared at the door, there was a roar from the crowd.

11. The *GPO Style Manual* presents the following on Army, Navy, and Air Force:

> U.S. Army, French Army; the Army, Army Establishments, Organized Reserves, the Volunteers, 1st Regiment, VII Corps, the Corps (U.S. understood in all cases). *But:* volunteer officer, army shoe, Lee's army, Robinson's brigade, the brigade, the regiment.
>
> U.S. Navy, British Navy; the Navy, Navy (or Naval) Establishment, Navy officers, the Marine Corps, the corps, the Marines, a marine.
>
> U.S. Air Force, Royal Air Force; Andrews Air Force Base, the base; Air Materiel Command, the command.

12. Capitalize the words *department, bureau, service, station, office, agency, commission,* and *board* if referring to a bureau or executive department of the U.S. Government when the name is given.

the Department of State	Newport Naval Station
the Bureau of Customs	the Foreign Service
the Federal Reserve Board	the Securities and
the Environmental	Exchange Commission
Protection Agency	

Business usage varies as to the capitalization of such words as *bureau, department, office,* and the like following a name.

Adjustment Bureau *or* adjustment bureau
Savings Department *or* savings department
Department of Applied Science *or* department of applied science
Employment Office *or* employment office

Do not capitalize *department, office, bureau,* and like words when used without a name or if used as an adjective.

I am going to the office.
He was employed by one of the Government bureaus.
The department clerk filed the report.

13. Capitalize *committee* with a name or in place of the name when referring to all standing and select committees of the Senate and the House of Representatives.

House Census Committee	Committee on Ways and Means

14. Capitalize *Federal* and *State Courts* when used with a definite name. Do not capitalize *city and county courts.*

the United States Supreme Court	the State Court of Appeals
the United States Circuit Court	Court of Claims
	the police court
	the magistrate's court

Capitalize *Court* when meaning a judge or judicial tribunal in direct personal reference to such a judge or tribunal.

15. Capitalize the word *Cabinet* when referring to the Cabinet of the President of the United States.

Cabinet officer
the President's Cabinet
the chief post of the Cabinet

16. Capitalize *Federal* when referring to the U.S. Government.

He was in the service of the Federal Government.

17. Usage varies as to the capitalization of *administration.* When referring to the political party in power or when used with a name to designate a Government board, *administration* is usually capitalized.

the Republican Administration
the Administration
the Reagan Administration
a former administration
Veterans' Administration

18. Capitalize *Government* when used synonymously with the U.S. Government or when referring to that of any foreign nation.

a Government official
Federal Government
National Government
Government ownership
the Italian Government

Imperial Government
Her Majesty's
   Government
a Government bureau

Do not capitalize *government* when referring to that of a state in the United States or to that of any possession of the United States.

19. Capitalize *commonwealth, confederation, powers, union,* etc., if used with proper names or as proper names or as proper adjectives.

Commonwealth of Massachusetts
Swiss Confederation
United Nations
Union of Soviet Socialist Republics

20. Capitalize *Consititution* when referring to that of the United States or to a specific national constitution.

James Madison was called the Father of the Constitution.
The Constitution of the United States of America was adopted in 1789.
The Constitutional Convention of Philadelphia set up the Federal Government of the United States.
Constitutional Committee, Constitutional Amendment

But: New York constitution

Also *act, bill, code, law, report,* and *treaty* with a name or number to designate a particular document are capitalized.

Smith Act
Bill of Rights
Internal Revenue Code
Public Law 9

Annual Report of the
   Secretary of Defense
Jay Treaty

21. Capitalize any U.S. Government *commission* when it is designated by its name.

Atomic Energy Commission
Commission of Fine Arts

Federal Communications Commission
Interstate Commerce Commission
Securities and Exchange Commission
U.S. Tariff Commission

Also capitalize *commission* when standing alone, if it refers to a national or international commission already named.

22. Capitalize all names of state legislatures when used with the name of the state and all names of national legislatures and their branches.

Florida Legislature
the Assembly of New York
the Ohio House of Representatives
the General Court of Massachusetts
the Eighty-ninth Congress
House of Commons
Chamber of Deputies
Rigsdag

But do not capitalize *assembly, general court, legislature*, if they stand alone without the name of the state to which they belong. Do not capitalize *national legislature*, meaning the United States Congress; or *city legislature*, meaning City Council or Board of Aldermen; or *executive session, special session*.

23. Capitalize *nation* and *republic* when used as a synonym for the United States or when used with a name to designate a definite nation.

These defense measures are essential to the safety of the Nation.
"With the election of this great statesman, the future of the Republic is assured," declared the chairman of the winning party.

But: Every nation in this hemisphere is invited to participate in the forthcoming conference.

Capitalize *national* when preceding a capitalized word.

National Capital
National Academy of Sciences
The National Government

But: national ideas, national pride, national anthem, a national monument
The national defense demands not merely force but intelligence.

24. Capitalize *state* when used with a name or when used in place of the name, but lower-case when used as a general term.

New York State	State government
the State of Ohio	State Democratic
the State leaders	headquarters
State ticket	

This State must cope with its own problems.

Note the usage of capitalization in the following examples:

state prison	Mountain States
states' rights	Southern States
State's attorney	Thirteen Original States
state's evidence	a foreign state

25. Capitalize the names of organized bodies and their adherents.

Republicans	Socialists
Shriners	Elks

Usage differs as to the capitalization of the word *party*.

the Communist Party *or* the Communist party

26. Capitalize names of clubs, associations, institutes, orders, companies, foundations, funds, groups, etc.

the Moravian Club	Knights of Columbus
The Macmillan Publishing Company	National Institutes of Health
Order of the Sacred Heart	the Cambridge Group
American Academy of Arts and Letters	American Association of University Women

Do not capitalize clubs, associations, institutes, orders, colleges, and the like when used alone, unless they have the value of a proper noun.

He belonged to a carpenters' union.
The clubs and associations of this city are numerous.
The Association voted on the question of dues.
The Board will meet on June 15.

27. Capitalize names of squares, parks, towers, monuments, statues, buildings, thoroughfares, churches.

Union Square	the Washington
the Tower of London	Monument *or* the
Park Row	Monument
Gramercy Park	the House (National)
the Mall	Halls of Congress
Eiffel Tower	the Capitol Grounds
the Capitol (Washington)	the Lincoln Memorial
Metropolitan Museum of	the Mormon Temple
Art	the Golden Gate Bridge
the Library of Congress	Capitol Halls of
Temple Emanu-el	Congress
Avery Library	Governor's Mansion
the Hall of Fame	Kingsway
the Executive Mansion	the Pennsylvania
Mansion House (London)	Turnpike
the Guild Theater	Capitol Chamber
the White House	Westminster Abbey
Statue of Liberty	Champs Elysées
Trinity Church	Rock Creek Park

But: the statue of Lincoln, the tomb of Washington

In some telephone and city directories, and in many newspapers, the words *avenue, street, boulevard, square, place,* and *court* are not written with initial capitals, even when used to indicate particular places. This style, however, is not recommended for use in correspondence and business writing.

The plural form of a common noun written as part of a proper noun is capitalized according to Government usage, but many publications advocate writing the plural form of the common noun without initial capital.

Capitalize a common noun when it is used as a well-known short form of a specific proper name.

the Canal (Panama Canal)   the Lakes (Great Lakes)

Place references when merely descriptive and preceded by *the* are not capitalized.

the mountains of North   the valley of the
   Carolina   Susquehanna

28. Capitalization of a geographical term follows various usages. The following rules and lists of terms have been adapted from *GPO Style Manual*.

(1) In business writing the following geographical terms are usually capitalized in the singular or plural, immediately following the name:

archipelago	gap	park
basin	glacier	passage
bend	gulch	peninsula
branch (stream)	harbor	plateau
butte	hill	point
canal	hollow	pond
channel	inlet	range (mountains)
cove	island	reef
crater	mesa	ridge
creek	mountain	run (stream)
current	narrows	shoal
flat(s)	ocean	sound

(2) In business writing the following words are usually capitalized, singular or plural, when they stand before a name or after it, or when they are used as a part of a name:

bay	mount
bayou	oasis
camp (military)	pass
cape	port (*but*, port of New
desert	York)

falls	river
fort	sea
head	strait
isle	valley
lake	

(3) Capitalize the following words if part of a name. Do not capitalize them when they are used in a general sense; as, the *rivers* of Maine, the *valleys* of California and North Carolina:

airport	gulf	rapids
beach	lagoon	reservation
borough	landing	reservoir
cavern	lighthouse	spring
ferry	plain	tunnel
forest	prairie	volcano
gorge	province	woods

(4) Do not capitalize the following terms, even when they are used with a name or a number:

breakwater	drydock	spillway
buoy	levee	watershed
chute	lock	weir
dike	pier	wharf
dock	slip	

29. Capitalize special names of countries or regions of countries, cities or sections of cities, rivers, bays, oceans, mountains, islands, and other geographical names.

Old World	the Tropics
New World	the Eternal City
Orient	the Left Bank (Paris)
Occident	the Hill (Capitol Hill,
Far East	Congress)
the Levant	the Southland
the Continent (*but*, the	Greater Seattle
continent of Europe)	the Loop
the Empire State	the North End (Boston)
the Middle West	the Sun Belt
the Northern Pacific States	the Lower East Side
the South Pole	(New York)
the Great Plains	the Delta

If a common noun or adjective forming an essential part of a name becomes removed from the rest of the name by an intervening common noun or adjective, the entire expression is no longer a proper noun and is therefore not capitalized.

Union Station, union passenger station
Eastern States, eastern farming states

30. Capitalize points of the compass when they designate geographical parts of the country.

Southern States	the Northwest
out West	Midwestern States

The South has increased its manufactures.
Election returns from the East are eagerly awaited.
The North took a decided stand on the question.
Big concentrated buying orders credited to Eastern sources were in evidence.

Do not capitalize such words when used merely to indicate direction.

—in Virginia and the colonies to the north and south of her.

facing south	north of Boston
driving east	west of the Rockies

(1) Do not capitalize adjectives derived from regional names when they are merely descriptive in character.

continental customs	oriental life
western hospitality	southern cooking
eastern fashions	northern climate
tropical fruits	an east wind

(2) Capitalize *northern, southern, western, eastern,* etc., when used as part of proper names to designate a world division; do not capitalize such words when used to indicate parts of states.

Central and Southwestern Europe	western New York
	eastern Pennsylvania

Eastern Asia
West South Africa
Eastern Hemisphere

southern California
northern Ohio
eastern Texas

(3) Nouns referring to the inhabitants of different sections of the United States may or may not be capitalized.

Northerner   *or*   northerner
Easterner   *or*   easterner

31. Capitalize all proper names denoting political divisions.

United Kingdom
French Republic
the Dominion of Canada
the Commonwealth of
  Massachusetts
the Republic (United
  States)
the South American
  Republics

the Papal States
Ward Ten
Nineteenth District
Fourth Precinct
Thirteenth Congressional
  District
Orange County
City of New York

32. Capitalize *college, uiniversity, seminary, school, high school,* etc., when used with a proper name. When such words are used alone, do not capitalize unless the word stands for a definite college or university and has the value of a proper name.

Elmira College
the College of Fine Arts
the School of Engineering
the Graduate School

Oak Park High School
Bacon Academy
Students Hall
Columbia University

33. Capitalize *church* when used with a name to designate a body of religious belief or a building and also when it designates the Church Universal; capitalize *cathedral, synagogue, temple,* and *chapel* when used with a name.

the Roman Catholic
  Church
the Church of England
High Church

the Cathedral of St. John
  the Divine
St. Patrick's Cathedral
the National Cathedral

Protestant Episcopal
  Church
the Presbyterian Church
the dignitaries of the
  Church
Church and State

Temple Emanu-el
Free Synagogue
Riverside Church
Harkness Chapel
the Unitarian Church

When *church, cathedral, synagogue, temple,* and *chapel* are used without a name or in a general sense, do not capitalize them.

church history
cathedrals of France
chapel exercises

synagogue services
the temple driveway

34. Capitalize all names for the Bible, for parts and versions of the Bible, and all names of other sacred books.

Bible
Scriptures
Holy Writ
Word of God
Holy Bible
Old Testament
New Testament
Pentateuch
the Ten Commandments
Gospels (*but,* gospel
  teachings)

Lord's Prayer
Twenty-third Psalm
Gospel of Mark
King James Version
Authorized Version
Vulgate
Revised Standard
  Version
Apocrypha
Koran
Talmud

Authorities differ regarding the capitalization of some adjectives derived from such nouns. The following examples are given in *The Random House Dictionary of the English Language:*

apocryphal
Biblical
rabbinical

scriptural
Talmudic
Vedic

35. Capitalize all names for the Deity.

Father
Almighty
Judge of Nations
Jehovah

Supreme Being
First Cause
Divine Providence
Lord of Hosts

Messiah the Comforter	Holy Spirit
Son of Man	Holy Trinity
King of the Jews	Redeemer
Holy Ghost	Savior

Do not capitalize *fatherhood, sonship, messiah-ship, messianic.*

36. Capitalize the *Virgin Mary*, the *Virgin*, the *Blessed Virgin*, *Madonna*, the *Holy Mother*, *Our Lady*.

37. In the Bible and in the Book of Common Prayer, pronouns relating to the Deity are not capitalized.

O Lord, thou hast been our dwelling-place in all generations.
And he looked up and saw the rich men that were casting their gifts into the treasury.

Opinions of publishers of other books differ in regard to the capitalization of pronouns relating to the Deity.

The nominative and the accusative of the personal pronouns—He and Him, Thou and Thee—are capitalized in this connection, but not the possessives, his and thine.

All pronouns referring to the Supreme Being, or any member of the Christian Trinity when closely preceded or followed by a distinct reference to the Deity, should be capitalized.

"Trust Him who rules all things" (*but:* "When God worked six days he rested the seventh").

38. Capitalize *Heaven* when referring to the Deity, and *Paradise* and *Heaven* only when referring to the hereafter; also *Hades*, but not *hell*.

Her prayers, whom Heaven delights to hear.

WILLIAM SHAKESPEARE

New thoughts of God, new hopes of Heaven.

JOHN KEBLE

But: Sharecropping, no heaven for the tenant, was no paradise for the farmer.

He descended into hell.

BOOK OF COMMON PRAYER

And in Hades, he lifted up his eyes, being in torment.

GOSPEL OF LUKE (REVISED STANDARD VERSION)

39. Capitalize the *Pope,* or the *Popes,* always; also *Holy Father, Pontiff,* and *Holiness,* meaning the Pope; *Cardinal, Apostolic Delegate, Archbishop, Bishop, Moderator,* and *Presiding Elder* before personal names; also when used separately after the person has been mentioned or when used in direct reference to persons holding office.

The New York Times Manual of Style and Usage

Every heart that has not been blinded and hardened by this terrible war must be touched by this moving appeal of his Holiness, the Pope.

WOODROW WILSON

40. Capitalize all names of creeds and confessions of faith and general Biblical terms.

the Apostles' Creed	the Westminster
Nicene Creed	Catechism
Canon Law	Thirty-nine Articles
Westminster Confession of	Lord's Supper
Faith	Creed of Pius IV
The New Testament	the Ten Commandments

41. Capitalize *Devil,* the *Evil One,* the *Adversary,* the *Father of Lies,* and *Beelzebub* meaning Satan.

And the great dragon was thrown down, that ancient serpent, who is called the Devil and Satan . . .

REVELATION 12:9 (REVISED STANDARD VERSION)

Do not capitalize when used in general sense or as an expletive.

42. Capitalize all names of holy days and holidays.

Christmas	Feast of Tabernacles
Easter	Whitsuntide
Good Friday	Memorial Day

Labor Day	New Year's Day
Yom Kippur	Thanksgiving Day
Fourth of July	All Saints' Day
Columbus Day	Michaelmas
Passover	Lincoln's Birthday

43. Capitalize the first word following a colon when it introduces an independent passage or sentence. (*See* p. 93.)

> A claim letter that makes unreasonable demands does one of two things: It antagonizes the recipient, or it convinces him that the grounds of complaint are unwarranted.

But do not capitalize a short list of words or phrases following colon directly.

> There are three steps of a century of educational development in America: industrialism, urbanization, mass schooling.

44. Capitalize the first word of each item in an outline:

> 1. Attracting attention
> 2. Creating desire
> 3. Convincing the mind
> 4. Stimulating action

45. Capitalize the first word of every complete quotation.

> The child cried, "Where is my new ball?"

(1) Do not capitalize the first word of a direct quotation when the quotation is introduced indirectly in the text.

> The governor called the explosion "a medical disaster and a legal quagmire."

(2) Do not capitalize that part of a quotation resumed within the same sentence.

> "Nature," said Lowell, "abhors the credit system."

(3) Capitalize the first word of a question made in direct form but not quoted.

The eighteenth century asked of a thing, Is it rational? The seventeenth century asked of a thing, Is it legal? or, when it went further, Is it according to conscience?

(4) Do not capitalize the first word of an indirect question or statement.

He asked what was the meaning of the party's steady growth in power.
Stevenson says that it is charm which is the basis of enduring art.

(5) Do not capitalize a partial quotation when this quotation is used as a motto on a title page or as a heading of a chapter; as,

... the cherished companion of my life, in whose affections, unabated on both sides, I had lived the last ten years in unchequered happiness.

THOMAS JEFFERSON

(6) Do not capitalize a parenthetical statement that occurs in the middle of a sentence.

The planes (all of them now out of date) were grounded.
The model he chose (she arrived as we were speaking) assumed a languid pose.

46. Capitalize the first word of exclamatory or of interrogative sentences used in a series.

O Rome! My country! City of the soul!

BYRON

Have you any idea what the habit of being loyal is worth? Do you know what it means to your happiness? To your success?

47. Capitalize *Whereas* and *Resolved* in resolutions and the first word following *Resolved.* A comma follows *Resolved.*

Whereas the United States Tariff Commission . . .
Resolved, That the Unitarian Universalist Association urges its member churches and fellowships to work for . . .

But: When *whereas* is written in full capitals, a comma follows:

WHEREAS, in order to preserve open space for the enjoyment of present and future generations . . .

48. Capitalize the article *the,* or its equivalent in a foreign language, when it is the authorized part of a geographical name, of a title of a book or of a work of art, or when incorporated as part of the legal name of a company or of an institution.

Geographical names: The Dalles, The Hague, The Netherlands, The Weirs, El Salvador, La Paz, Le Havre; *but,* the Gulf States, the Midwest, the Orient, the Western Hemisphere.

Titles: *The Nine Tailors, The Bartered Bride, My Life in Art.*

Names of companies or institutions: The Federal Sugar Refining Company, The English-Speaking Union.

This rule is usually disregarded in newspapers and in informal writing when mentioning periodicals, ships, firm names, etc., as, the *Atlantic Monthly,* the *Olympia,* the Carborundum Company.

When used with personal titles if it is not the first word in a sentence, *the* should not be capitalized.

Two new ex-officio members of the Board were the Reverend Joseph O'Donnell and the Honorable James Ryan.

49. Capitalize references to divisions of a work when referred to in the same work.

See Chapter 4 in Part II.
Definitions will be found in the Glossary.

Do not capitalize these when used in a general sense; as,

We learned how to make an index.

50. Capitalize the names of the seasons only when they are personified.

If Winter comes, can Spring be far behind?
PERCY BYSSHE SHELLEY

We are going in the spring.

51. Personifications of abstract ideas or objects are sometimes capitalized.

In the name of Reason, will you please consider the results of such actions.
It has been said that Man proposes, God disposes.

But: It is not reason but habit which usually prevails.

52. Capitalize the names and synonyms for flags of nations: the Star-Spangled Banner, Old Glory, the National Emblem, the Union Jack.

53. In typewritten work, such as business letters and reports, when a noun is followed by a code reference or by a number, the word is ordinarily capitalized. When used generally, such words are not capitalized. The word *number* and its abbreviation *No.* are always omitted after *Form.*

Bulletin CL-50, a new bulletin
Catalogue B-4, our recent catalogue
Form 1040A, a shortened form
Contract No. 65, a long-term contract

54. Capitalize nouns followed by a capitalized Roman numeral.

Act I, Vol. V, Book II

Often *in references* such nouns and Roman numerals are not capitalized.

Subdivisions and their abbreviations in literary references are not capitalized.

article—art.	line—l.	page—p.	verse—vs.
chapter— chap.	note—n.	section—sec.	volume—vol.

55. Capitalize all principal words (that is, nouns, pronouns, adjectives, adverbs, verbs, and first words) in titles of books, pictures, plays, radio programs, television shows, musical compositions, documents, reports, papers, proceedings, captions, display lines, headings. (*See* pages 121–23 for use of italics with various kinds of titles.)

Books:	*Lake Wobegon Days*
	Handling Executive Stress
Pictures:	a print of "American Gothic"
	Da Vinci's "Last Supper"
Radio programs:	*Sportsnight with Jack Spector*
	All Things Considered
Television shows:	*Hill Street Blues*
	Masterpiece Theater
Musical Compositions:	Stravinsky's *Firebird*
	The Grand Canyon Suite
	Chopin's Nocturne, Opus 37, No. 2
	"The Star-Spangled Banner"
Documents, Reports, and Proceedings:	U.S. Constitution
	Report of the Special Committee on Immigration
	Proceedings of the Fifth Annual Conference on Learning Disabilities
Captions:	Sampling Fine Wines of the Valley
	Foreign Equities Gain Favor

In informal usage in letters and advertisements book titles may be given in full caps.

I have enjoyed reading THE GREENER GRASS.

56. Capitalize scientific names of the world's eras, common names for historical epochs, periods in the history of literature or language, and important events.

the Neolithic age   the Wars of the Roses
the Paleozoic period   Colonial days

the Fourth Glacial age	Revolutionary period
the Christian Era	the days of the Second
the Crusades	Empire
the Middle Ages	the Louisiana Purchase
the Renaissance	the Battle of Bull Run

57. Capitalize all names of the bodies of the solar system except for *earth, moon, stars,* and *sun* (unless they are personified or used in an astronomical context).

the Milky Way	Orion
the Great Bear	Cassiopeia's Chair
the Big Dipper	the North Star
Venus	the Southern Cross

58. Capitalize in botanical, geological, zoological, and paleontological matter the scientific (Latin) names of divisions, orders, families, and genera, but not their English derivatives.

> Cotylosauria, *but* cotylosaurs
> Cruciferae, *but* crucifers

59. In botanical, geological, zoological, paleontological, and medical matter the names of species are never capitalized.

Cedrus libani	*Styrax californica*
Felis leo	*Conodectes favosus*
Cocos nucifera	*Epigaea repens*

60. Do not capitalize abbreviations unless the words they represent are usually capitalized, as, *F.* or *Fahr.* (*Fahrenheit*) or *C.* (*Celsius*); or unless the abbreviation has been capitalized by custom, as *ETA* (*estimated time of arrival*) or *No.* (*number*).

61. Abbreviations for forenoon and afternoon may be written as follows:

> a.m. *or* A.M.
> p.m. *or* P.M.

62. Do not capitalize units of measurement such as *6 ft., 4 lbs., 3 qts.*

63. Capitalize the trade names of manufactured products, but lower-case the words following a trade name that are not part of the name.

Bon Ami	Celotex	Pet milk	Goodyear tires

64. Capitalize most adjectives formed from proper nouns. Do not capitalize such adjectives in French, Italian, Norwegian, Spanish, and Swedish text.

Arabic	Nipponese
British	Olympian
Canadian	Pan-American
Chesterfieldian	Papal
Elizabethan	Parisian
Gregorian	Rooseveltian
Hellenic	Semitic
Latin	Swiss
Napoleonic	Victorian

65. In advertising and in journalistic writing, capitals are often used for emphasis. This should be done sparingly, as excessive capitalization tends to weaken rather than to emphasize.

66. Capitalize both parts of a hyphenated word if each part is ordinarily capitalized: *Anglo-American* attitude, *Scotch-Irish* ancestry. When a prefix that is part of a hyphenated word is ordinarily written without a capital, it is not capitalized when combined with a proper noun except when used as the name of an organization or in a title that would require capitalization.

anti-American	non-Swedish
intra-European	trans-Canadian

but

Inter-American Artists	Trans-Siberian Railway

While authorities differ on the capitalization of hyphenated words in titles and headings, the following rule is generally accepted:

In titles and headings, capitalize words that form parts of hyphenated compounds without regard for hyphens.

New Do-It-Yourself Landscaping Guide
Test-Tube Plants Assure Virus-Free Strawberries
How to Make an Ice-Cream Drive-In Pay

67. A list of words and expressions showing their generally accepted capitalization follows. Note that some words derived from proper nouns have developed a special meaning; these words are no longer capitalized.

afghan (lap robe)
Afghan hound
Allies (World Wars I & II)
American history
Americanization
anglicize
Anglo-French entente
artesian well
bologna sausage
boycott
braille
brussels sprouts
cesarean section
Cheshire cheese
chinaware
delftware
English literature
French château
french dressing
Georgian architecture
Gothic architecture
gothic novel
Grades I–XII
Icelandic legends
india ink
Indian corn
lyonnaise potatoes
macadamized road
madras cloth

melba toast
mercurial
mid-Atlantic
morocco leather
oxford shoe
plaster of paris
Pompeian red
poor whites
portland cement
pro-British
Province of Quebec
Puritan colony
puritanical ethics
Roman citizens
roman type
Room 224
russian dressing
Russian olive
spanish omelet
Statement No. 2
Table No. 5
transatlantic
transoceanic
tropical fruits
the tropics
un-American
Wedgwood ware
X ray (noun)
x-ray (verb)

Punctuation

The Period

1. Place a period at the end of a declarative sentence, at the end of an indirect question, and at the end of an imperative sentence that does not express strong emotion.

   Green belts around cities are attractive and provide oxygen.
   He could not determine why the changes had not been made.
   Leave two lines blank below your name and address.

2. Place a period after a request. A question mark is not used when a request or order is implied.

   Will you please sign and return the application.
   May I have your opinion of this proposal.

3. Place a period after an abbreviation that stands for a single word. (*See also* Rules 5 and 6.)

   John Smith and Co., Inc.   Mrs. Susan Richards
   the first century A.D.   Jan. 6

   However, the trend is to eliminate periods in abbreviations, especially in units of all kinds.

lb	*or*	lb.		mph	*or*	m.p.h.
hr	*or*	hr.		mpg	*or*	m.p.g.
oz	*or*	oz.		yd	*or*	yd.

   Note the uses of the period after an abbreviation in connection with other punctuation marks.

(1) When the last word in a sentence is abbreviated, one period will suffice.

We plan to meet at 9 A.M.

(2) Before a colon:

These instructions came from Cox & Box Ltd: Never use chemicals on the lens; use only mild soap and water.

(3) Before a semicolon:

The gardens are open from 9 A.M. to dusk daily, May–Sept.; 10 A.M. to 5 P.M., Oct.–April.

4. Do not place a period after *Mme* and *Mlle* in French (American usage, *Mme.* and *Mlle.*); after abbreviations of well-known publications, as *PMLA* (Publications of the Modern Language Association); or after abbreviations for linguistic epochs, as *OE* (Old English), *MHG* (Middle High German).

5. Ordinarily do not place a period between letters indicating the names of government boards, commissions, and services; as, *AEC, FBI, TVA;* or after the call letters of broadcasting stations: *CBS, NBC, WTOP.*

6. According to individual preference, periods may or may not be placed after initials representing full personal names; as *R. L. S., T. R., F. D. R.* or *RLS, TR, FDR.*
   In monograms periods are always omitted.

OWR   BI

In indicating the initials of a person dictating a letter and those of the typist, periods are always omitted.

AJ:STM   LPD:jb   lpd:jb

7. Do not place a period after Roman numerals unless in a table of contents or in lists.

Vol. X   Elizabeth II   John Delano III

I. Preparation of Content of Report
II. Arrangement of Content
III. Typing the Report

8. Do not place a period after letters when they refer to a person; as, *Mr. A* has paid his monthly common charges.

9. Place periods after letters or figures in an outline when they mark the chief division of a subject. Omit the periods when the letters or figures are enclosed in parentheses.

I.
    A.
    B.
        1.
        2.
            a.
            b.
            c.
                (1)
                (2)
                    (a)
                    (b)
II. etc.

10. Place a period before a decimal.

$20.38   .05   12.6   .31416

11. A period may be used between figures denoting hours and minutes; as, 10.15. However, the colon is generally used; as, 10:15. (*See* p. 93.)

12. Place the period inside the parentheses when they enclose an independent sentence. (*See* pp. 106–107.)

The firm was incorporated a few years ago. (I am not sure just when.)

13. Place the period outside the parentheses when the enclosed matter forms part of the preceding statement and is not an independent statement.

These campaign techniques proved effective (so the experts decreed, though they could offer no proof).
Orders were placed for F-14 and F-15 aircraft (then still in development).

14. **Place a period inside quotation marks.**(*See* p. 102.)

I am going to read Tomlinson's "Gifts of Fortune."
Do not use such expressions as "Best on the market."

15. Omit the period after all display lines; after running heads; after centered headlines; after side-heads set in separate lines; after cut-in heads; after box-heads in tables; after superscriptions and legends that do not make more than a single line of type; after items in enumerated lists; after date lines heading communications; and after signatures.

However, if one item in a list is a complete sentence, a period is used. In that case, all items are followed by a period.

16. Do not place a period after chemical symbols, the words indicating size of books, or the word "percent."

H_2O 16mo   10 percent

17. Omit the period after a signature and after a title following a signature in a letter.

Yours very truly,
Martha Alexander
Personnel Director

18. Use three periods separated by spaces to denote an omission in quoted matter. When the omission occurs at the end of a sentence, the sentence period is retained as well. Use seven periods spaced across the page to denote the omission of one or more paragraphs of quoted matter.

Henry Clay declared that the veto is totally irreconcilable with the genius of representative government if it is . . . employed with respect to the expediency of measures, as well as their constitutionality.

The Comma

1. Use a comma to separate words and phrases in a series.

> When the electricity fails, there's no elevator, no light, no television, none of the amenities.

> The comma causes trouble equally by its absence, by its presence, and by wrong placement.
> WILSON FOLLETT, *Modern American Usage*

> Business positions differ greatly in the training required, in the opportunities for advancement, and in the financial rewards.

> From the campuses has come the expertise to travel to the moon, to crack the genetic code, and to develop computers that calculate as fast as light.

> Sharing in the indicated larger yields were corn, potatoes, apples, tobacco, and peanuts.

Present usage advocates the use of the comma before *and* connecting the last two words of a series; some writers, however, prefer to omit the comma before *and*.

(1) Do not use a comma when the conjunction connects all the words in a series.

> Reading and writing and 'rithmetic are still basic.

(2) When *etc.* ends a series, it should be preceded and followed by a comma. (*Etc.* is, of course, the abbreviation of *et cetera,* and since *et* means *and,* the word *and* should not precede *etc.*)

> Last week a sale of chairs, beds, desks, etc., was advertised by Law & Dutton.

(3) In company names consisting of a series of surnames, most organizations omit the comma between the last two members: *Hudson, Blair & Grant; Lawrence, Stevenson and Kane.* When the word *company*

completes the series, the comma is omitted: *Green, Lake and Company.*

2. Use a comma between adjectives preceding a noun when they are coordinate qualifying words.

   The managers agreed on a form for a shortened, simplified, uniform report.

   Do not use a comma between two adjectives preceding a noun if using the comma destroys the intended relationship, since the adjectives are too closely related to be separated.

additional reasonable cost	huge boxlike building
quaint old mining town	outstanding military service

3. Use a comma to separate pairs of words in a series.

   Official and nonofficial, national and state agencies attended the convention in Boston.

4. Use a comma or commas to separate the name of the person addressed or his/her title from the rest of the sentence.

   I suppose, Mrs. Harrison, that this is your final offer.
   We are glad to welcome you, Captain Bligh.
   Well, Professor, this is the first I have heard of the idea.

5. Use a comma to set off words in apposition.

   Martha L. Ferris, chairman of Consolidated Amalgams, has announced the merger.
   The minimum daily requirement of minerals, such as iron, zinc, calcium, and manganese, differs among species.

6. Do not separate compound personal pronouns from the words they emphasize.

   Bruce himself sent the telegram.
   The members themselves will make up the deficit.

7. Do not use commas when a word or phrase is in italics or enclosed in quotation marks.

The word *caprice* is derived from the Latin word *caper*.
A little south of the "northern tier" barrier reef . . .

8. Omit the comma when an appositive has become part of a proper name.

   Eric the Red   William the Conqueror

9. Omit the comma when the connection is unusually close between an appositive and the word it modifies.

   Our salesman Brown covers the New England territory.

   But: Our salesman, Herbert Brown, covers the New England territory.

10. Use a comma to set off inverted names in bibliographies, in indexes, in directories, or in other reference lists.

    Cleveland, Orford B.   Babineau, Celeau
    Rabinowitz, Melvin, D.C.   Laszlo, Stephen, M.D.

11. Use a comma to separate a name from a title or degree that follows it.

    Arthur Brookins Cudworth, dean of McGrath Law School
    Nijland S. Andersen, Ph.D.

    A comma may or may not be used before and after *Jr.* and *Sr.* following a name.

    John Lyons, Jr., presided.
    John Lyons Jr. presided.

    Omit periods and commas before and after II, III, and IV with names.

    Henry Lord III conducted the meeting.

12. Use a comma to set off a contrasted word, phrase, or clause.

    Saving, not spending, is the way of security.
    It is important for drivers to be vigilant, not heedless.
    The effective writer aims not at broad target areas, but at bull's-eyes.

13. Use a comma to set off a transitional word or expression; as, *then, indeed, nevertheless, moreover, of course,* when a pause is needed for clearness or for emphasis.

Indeed, we all considered the matter closed.
On the contrary, a college degree does not guarantee employability.
Nevertheless, he found himself at a loss for words.
She intended, as a matter of fact, to double the plant's output in six months' time.
The more you travel, obviously, the easier you should find it to adjust to other people's customs.
Knowing one's limitations may, it is true, discourage one from trying new ways.

When such parenthetical words, phrases, and clauses do not interrupt the thought or require punctuation for clearness, the commas should be omitted.

The jury therefore gave a unanimous decision.
We are accordingly signing the contract.
It is indeed strange that so few children read well today.
The decision in this case is probably not significant.

14. Use a comma to indicate the omission of a word, usually a word that has been used before in the sentence.

Common stocks are preferred by some investors; bonds, by others; and mortgages, by still others.

Often, however, commas are omitted if the meaning is clear without them.

The Englishman's virtue is wisdom; the Frenchman's is reason; the Spaniard's serenity.

15. A comma should follow *yes, no, why, well* when one of these words is used at the beginning of a sentence.

Why, we expected him to be appointed district manager this year.
Well, the decision has been made and we have to live with it.

But: When *well* or *why* is used as an adverb, no comma is needed.

However well he played, his teacher failed to encourage him.
We could not determine why the machine stopped suddenly.

16. Use a comma to set off light exclamations.

Oh, a change would be nice, but I can't afford a vacation just now.
Heavens, I never expected to be taken so seriously.

17. Use a comma to set off a phrase denoting residence or position but not before ZIP Code numbers.

Alexander Vanderpoll, a resident of Larchmont (N.Y.), addressed the meeting.
Address the letter to Mr. Alexander Vanderpoll, President of the Dandy Popcorn Company, 5 Cliff Way, Larchmont, NY 10538.

18. Use a comma in dates.

The University of Southern North Dakota was founded at Hoople on April 1, 1958.

A comma may be used to separate the month from the year when the date is omitted, as *June, 1982;* current usage, however, permits *June 1982.*

Record temperatures were set in June 1982 in New York.

19. Use a comma to set off figures in groups of more than four digits, as 1,000,000. (*See* p. 124.)

20. Use a comma to separate two figures or words indicating figures in order to make their meaning clear.

On November 14, 379 stocks closed at the highest for the year.
Instead of thousands, millions were spent.

21. If such introductory words as *as, for example, for instance, namely, viz., that is* and the terms following form parenthetical expressions and do not introduce enumerations, a comma precedes and follows the introductory word. (*See* pp. 90–91 for use of semicolon and p. 92 for use of colon.)

> Many smaller universities, for example, Pace and Sacred Heart, have instituted courses in business administration.
> You know that our November holiday, that is, Thanksgiving, was a New England institution.
> Perhaps the most important factor of all is the psychological one, namely, the glamour of aviation, for the Armed Forces never lack for volunteers in this branch.

The use of the comma after *e.g.* (*exempli gratia*, for example) and *i.e.* (*id est*, that is) is optional. The present tendency is to omit the comma.

22. The use of the comma after phrases and clauses at the beginning of a sentence is not an arbitrary requirement.

(1) Use a comma after a long introductory prepositional phrase out of its natural order or when punctuation is needed for clearness.

> In regard to the cost of remodeling your home, it is likely to be more economical than buying another house at present interest rates.
> Besides having to buy a car, he needed to find a place to live.
> For the billing department, new procedures were to be implemented as quickly as possible.

But usually short introductory prepositional phrases need not be followed by a comma, except when they are distinctly parenthetical; as, *for example, in fact, on the other hand.*

> In recent months many changes have taken place in the city.
> During the last twenty years the company's profits have tripled.
> On Saturday the offices are closed.

(2) Use a comma after introductory participial and absolute phrases.

The matter being decided, the President continued his report.
Realizing the need for more storage room, we built a new wing.
Generally speaking, his successes go unnoticed.
All things considered, the decision was just.

(3) Use commas to set off nonrestrictive participial phrases. A nonrestrictive participial phrase adds an additional thought and might be omitted without interfering with the meaning.

The letter from the Brooks Company, just received by Collins, clarifies the problem.

(4) Do not use a comma to set off restrictive participial phrases. A restrictive participial phrase is essential to the meaning of the sentence.

All persons known to have seen the accident will be questioned.

(5) Use commas to set off descriptive phrases following the noun they modify.

The stock, having reached 175, remained there for three weeks.
The child, pale with fatigue, waited for her mother.

23. When a dependent adverbial clause precedes a main clause, a comma is generally used.

While the general trend has been upward, decreases in the tax rates are not unknown.
Before the sale is advertised, we must take an inventory of our present stock.

But a short introductory adverbial clause may need no comma after it, if there is no uncertainty where the main clause begins; this is likely to be the case when the subject of both clauses is the same.

If we go back in American history we find this country has never kept silence as to what it stands for.
Before I began to write novels I had forgotten all I learned at school and college.

Note that when the dependent clause follows the main clause, the comma is usually omitted, except when the clause is plainly nonrestrictive, that is, adds a reason or concession introduced by *because, since, as, though.*

He was always at hand when there was difficult work to do.

He saw that some causes of international jealousy and of war would be removed if the grosser forms of exploitation of labor and the more distressing kinds of competition in this field . . . were eliminated.

Loyalty is one of the cardinal virtues of a secretary, because of the confidential nature of the position.

24. Use a comma between the parts of a short compound sentence when punctuation is needed for clearness or to give an additional idea. (*See* p. 88 for use of semicolon.)

We have been planning this expansion for years, and I am glad the time has come to make a start.

But: Do not use commas to separate the members of a compound sentence when the clauses are short and closely related.

Fill in the enclosed blank and mail it today.

Distinguish between a compound sentence (two or more independent clauses) and a simple sentence with a compound predicate (two or more verbs with the same subject). Do not use a comma between the verbs of a compound predicate.

He joined the firm as an accountant and in time became manager.

They changed their plans and set up a dummy corporation.

25. Use a comma to separate similar or identical words standing next to each other, even when the sense or continuity does not seem to require it.

Whatever is, is right.   Whenever you go, go quickly.

26. Use a comma to set off a nonrestrictive adjective clause. Such a clause is one that is not needed to make the meaning clear.

> Engraved stationery, which conveys the impression of dignity and reliability, adds to the attractiveness of correspondence.
>
> Dr. Saul Grossman, who is regarded as one of the leading theorists in the study of anorexia, will address the meeting.

27. Do not use a comma to set off a restrictive adjective clause. Such a clause is one that is needed to make the meaning clear.

> Many of the sales are made to people who are footloose or retired and who see in the mobile home a means of dispensing with the problems of ordinary home ownership.
>
> Anyone who has not learned to appreciate classical music is unfortunate.

Present usage generally favors *which* when the relative clause conveys a qualification or statement simply additional or parenthetic, and *that* when it is definitely restrictive.

> Our advertisements, *which* we strive to make truthful and convincing, have increased our business enormously this year.
>
> We keep books *that* are valuable in locked cases.
>
> All material *that* is on sale has been reduced in price.

28. Use a comma to set off informal direct quotations.

> "Wherever I am needed," declared the volunteer, "there I will gladly go."
>
> The doctor remarked, "I haven't seen many cases like yours as yet this season."
>
> "Let us reason together," I urged.

Note that no comma is needed in an indirect quotation.

> The supervisor told us all that chronic absenteeism would not be tolerated.
>
> We asked what the price for the larger refrigerator would be during Saturday's sale.
>
> Experience has shown how best to manage exit interviews.

29. Use a comma to set off words, phrases, and clauses that would otherwise be unclear.

> Wrong: This ticket is good for dinner or bed and breakfast.
> Right: This ticket is good for dinner, or bed and breakfast.
> Wrong: When I was about to begin the speech ended.
> Right: When I was about to begin, the speech ended.

30. For use of the comma with parentheses, *see* p. 107.

31. Omit the comma before the ZIP Code number in an address on an envelope; place the number two spaces after the two-letter state abbreviation.

The Semicolon

While the comma is frequently used in place of the semicolon in business letters, newspapers, and magazines, the semicolon has a place in modern writing. The following are the generally accepted rules for the use of the semicolon.

1. Use a semicolon between the clauses of a compound sentence when the conjunction is omitted or when the connection is not close.

> The Working Girl, long harassed and patronized, has earned her way to linguistic equality; a sign of the changing times is that it is not possible to say that Heaven protects the Career Woman.
>
> WILLIAM SAFIRE, *On Language*

The statistical evidence is there; it cannot be denied.

> I had no flair for politics as an art form; my interest was solely in the content of the candidate's message.
>
> GEORGE BALL

2. Use a semicolon to separate coordinate clauses when they are long or when they contain commas.

> The good modern letterwriter does not employ hackneyed expressions, for they make letters sound boring, lacking in in-

dividuality; they deprive letters of personal flavor; they clog the message, blur the meaning, confuse the construction.

We are not happy simply being useful; we want to identify with something, and thus we have courses on creative writing, creative advertising, and creative salesmanship.

J. S. BRUNER

3. Use the semicolon in lists of names with titles or addresses and in other lists that would not be clear if separated by commas.

Other speakers on the program were L. R. Alderman, Specialist in Adult Education in the U.S. Bureau of Education; Miss Willie Lawson, Deputy State Superintendent of Public Schools, Little Rock, AR; and Reed Lewis, Director of Foreign Language Information Service, New York City.

Officers elected for the coming year are as follows: president, James Thomas; secretary, Raymond Colt; treasurer, Kenneth Graham.

The survey was made in Hartford, Torrington, and Winsted in Connecticut; and in Springfield, Worcester, and Boston in Massachusetts.

Invitations to the dedication should be sent to Mrs. Burton Allen, 11 Lake Road, Newton Centre, MA; Miss Helen Wollaston, 26 Adelaide Avenue, Barrington, RI; and Dr. Luke Randall, Pleasant Valley, CT.

Horton's experience, according to his letter, has been two years as salesman for Bradford & Crane, Orlando, FL; four years as sales manager for The Norton Company, Kansas City, MO; and five years as buyer for Hall Brothers, Richmond, VA.

Where there would be no confusion, the comma may be used instead of the semicolon.

Regional offices are located in New York, NY, Chicago, IL, and Dallas, TX.

In lists of books with specific references to volume number, chapter number, pages, etc. (often given in footnotes to speeches, reports, or articles), each complete item should be separated by a semicolon.

Political Conditions in the South in 1868: Dunning, *Reconstruction, Political and Economic* (American Nation Series), pp. 109–123; Hart, *American History Told by Contemporaries*, Vol. IV, pp. 445–458, 497–500; Elson, *History of the United States*, pp. 790–805.

Psalms 23:1–4; 37:2–5; 91:1–10.

4. Use a semicolon to separate groups of words, whether phrases or clauses, dependent on a general term or statement.

He declared that physical exercise has many benefits: it strengthens the muscles of the legs; it increases the flow of blood throughout the body; it improves the appetite; and it helps to prevent osteoporosis.

We hold these truths to be self-evident—that all men are created equal; that they are endowed by their Creator with certain inalienable rights; that among these are life, liberty, and the pursuit of happiness.

THOMAS JEFFERSON

5. Use a semicolon to precede *for example, namely, for instance, viz., to wit, as, i.e.* when they introduce an enumeration of examples not felt to be parenthetical or when they precede a principal statement or a sentence. (*See* pp. 83–84 for use of comma, and p. 92 for use of colon.)

The examinations will include practical demonstrations of professional skills in actual life situations; for example, a secretary in an actual office situation, a teacher in an actual classroom, and a nurse with an actual patient.

Before purchasing a condominium, a buyer should consider a number of aspects; namely, location, construction quality, and financing.

[A stampede of cattle] could not be foretold; anything might start it; for instance, the sudden bark of a coyote, a rumble of a summer storm, lightning, the rearing of a horse, or the scream of a panther could all set off a disastrous stampede.

HORAN and SANN, *Pictorial History of the Wild West*

6. Use a semicolon to separate clauses joined by such transitional words as *hence, moreover, however, also, therefore, consequently.* Follow these words by commas when they themselves should be emphasized.

The principles are almost universally accepted; hence you should learn them.
The speaker saw no objection to the suggestion; therefore, she accepted it.

7. Use a semicolon to separate lengthy statements following a colon.

Amos Rapoport in *House Form and Culture* supports this view when he carefully lists three categories of architecture: 1. primitive—built with few modifications by all people on a common model; 2. vernacular—divided into preindustrial, which is built by tradesmen on a model that comes from the people (folk art), and post-industrial, built by specialists, from a model for the people (mass-culture art); and 3. highstyle—built by specialists (architects) for an elite cultural group.

ROBERT L. VICKERY, JR., *Sharing Architecture*

8. Place a semicolon outside quotation marks. (*See also* p. 103.)

We called him "Lucky"; he preferred "Lawrence."
"Infer" means "conclude"; "imply" means "suggest."

9. Place a semicolon after the parentheses when the parenthetical matter explains something that precedes.

What we are actually discussing here is the Planned Unit Development (PUD as it is called within the development profession); which is a large assemblage of land, usually 100 acres or more, in which single-family houses are mixed with higher density apartments and are clustered around cul-de-sacs.

ROBERT L. VICKERY, JR., *Sharing Architecture*

The Colon

1. Use a colon to introduce a list, or to introduce formally a statement, an enumeration, or an illustration.

> By mid-1942 various modifications [of the Selective Service Act] were introduced: All males between eighteen and sixty-five were required to be registered; the lottery was discarded and registrants were called by order of date of birth; voluntary enlistments were severely restricted . . .
>
> CALABRESI & BOBBITT, *Tragic Choices*

> Suggested accompaniments for sweet breads and rolls are:
> 1. Flavored sugars
> 2. Flavored butters
> 3. Glazes (frostings)

When such introductory expressions as *namely, for example, for instance* are omitted before a list, a colon is used.

> There were three reasons for his failure: laziness, ill health, and lack of training.

When the enumeration is informal or closely connected with the verb, the colon should be omitted.

> Children need food, shelter, love, and education.
> The early settlers were forced to clear land, plant crops, fish, and hunt game in order to survive.

2. Use a colon to introduce a formal or long quotation.

> The director gave the requirements for residence:
> Each resident must be able to care for her/himself.
> The cost of two meals per day and maid service every other week are included in the rent.
> Rent is payable on the first day of the month.
> Each resident must have a relative or other responsible person who will be called upon to make important decisions in the event the resident is unable to do so.

3. Use a colon after a formal salutation in a letter.

> Dear Sir: Gentlemen: Dear Madam:

4. A colon is sometimes used instead of a comma after the place of publication in bibliographical matter:

Stassinopoulos, Arianna. *Maria Callas: The Woman Behind the Legend.* New York: Simon and Schuster, 1981.

5. A colon is often used in the title of a magazine article or book, as in the previous example.

Jazz Lives: Portraits in Words and Pictures

6. Use a colon preceding a restatement of an idea.

The sentence was poorly constructed: it lacked both unity and coherence.

7. A colon is often used to precede an extended explanation.

True democracy presupposes two conditions: first, that the vast majority of the people have a genuine opinion upon public affairs; secondly, that electors will use their power as a public benefit.

ANDRE SIEGFRIED

8. Capitalize the first word following a colon when it introduces an independent passage or sentence. Do not capitalize the first word following a colon when it introduces an explanatory element or one logically dependent on what precedes.

The director gave these instructions: "Arrive on time, come regularly, telephone if you are too ill to come in, and take only one hour for lunch."

[Sourdough breads] rightly belong to the Far West: the old-time mountain men, sheepherders, prospectors, and miners.

DOLORES CASELLA, *A World of Breads*

9. A colon may be placed between figures denoting hours and minutes; as, 2:30. (*See* pp. 77 *and* 128.)

10. When a colon follows an abbreviation of two words (such as *i.e.* or *A.M.*), do not place a period after the abbreviation.

Our morning routine may vary, i.e: some days we hike two miles before breakfast, and other days we work out at the gym after we leave the office.
We expect delivery of the merchandise by 5 P.M: no later, earlier if possible.

The Question Mark

1. Use a question mark at the end of a direct question.

> One must always ask, Does this open space lead to a school or playground? To shopping or to community activity?
>
> ROBERT L. VICKERY, JR., *Sharing Architecture*

"Where can one find someone with the qualifications we need on our board?" asked the chairman.

An indirect question is followed by a period.

The chairman asked where one could find someone with the qualifications we need on our board.

A request is usually followed by a period, rather than by a question mark. (*See* p. 75.)

May I ask you to come early on Friday morning.
Would you mind letting me know whether or not he is still with the company.
Will you please look into this matter and let us have your comments.

2. When an emphatic question occurs within a sentence and is not a direct quotation, use a question mark.

Will advertising to such an extent pay? is a question.
But the real question is: How can our community afford to permit maintenance of school buildings to be delayed or overlooked?

When the question is not emphatic, a comma is generally used instead of a question mark.

How can such heavy expenditures be met, is a question that the administration must consider.

His main test for a salesman is, Will he create goodwill for the company, What kind of impression will he make?

3. Use a question mark after a quoted question at the end of a sentence.

The subject he will discuss is "How can credit be controlled?"

4. Use a question mark to indicate the end of a parenthetical question.

They wanted to know (would you believe it?) if the plane went nonstop from San Francisco to Honolulu.
The employees were pleased (who would not have been?) to be given an extra day off each month when the plant's quota had been filled.

5. A question mark in parentheses is sometimes used to indicate doubt or irony.

The present City Hall dates from 1758 (?).
The high point (?) of the evening came when the door prizes were awarded.
He provided documentation (?) of an earlier discovery by Norsemen.

6. Place the question mark inside the quotation marks when it belongs to the quoted matter.

"I know you can't tell now," she said, "but will you please call when you find the answer?"
The treasurer asked, "What will be the departmental budget for travel next year?"

But place the question mark outside the quotation marks when it is not a part of the quoted matter.

Do you agree to "Out of sight, out of mind"?
Who was it that said, "It ain't over till it's over"?

7. Use a question mark to express more than one question in the same sentence.

To judge a story or a motion picture, ask yourself the following questions: Is it realistic? romantic? whimsical? possible but not probable? Does the action get off to a fast start? How is suspense maintained?

The Exclamation Point

1. Use an exclamation point to mark an exclamatory word, phrase, or sentence.

   "The very thought of such a catastrophe is appalling!" declared the manager.
   Where in the world have you been! Just look at your clothes!
   What a magnificent achievement!

2. If the whole sentence is exclamatory in form, place an exclamation point at the end.

   How complicated these registration forms are!

3. Use an exclamation point at the end of sentences that are interrogatory in form but exclamatory in meaning.

   Is this the best that you can do after years of lessons!
   Now, I ask you, is that fair!
   Wouldn't you think he could hang up his own coat!

4. When an exclamation is not emphatic, place a comma instead of an exclamation point after it.

   "So this is all you have to offer, is it," said Joe, "and I'm expected to make the best of it."

5. Use an exclamation point to express irony, surprise, and dissension.

   Imagine a city without garbage!
   The doctor said my anxiety about being left alone is really a childish fear!

6. An exclamation point is used after a command.

   Ready, set, *go!*
   This is what I want done, and *now!*
   Call the fire department!

The Apostrophe

1. To form the possessive singular of nouns, add an apostrophe and *s* (*'s*): the *woman's* child, the *secre-*

tary's report, the *professor's* book, the *witness's* testimony.

2. To form the possessive singular of compound nouns, add an apostrophe and *s* (*'s*) at the end of the word: his *daughter-in-law's* manners, the *vice-consul's* arrival, a *letter carrier's* appointment.

3. To form the possessive singular of expressions used as compound nouns, add an apostrophe and *s* (*'s*) to the last word of an expression: *Charles the First's* failure, *Peter Miller Jr.'s* education, the *Duke of York's* palace.

4. To denote the possessive when a phrase is regarded as a compound noun and means a person or persons, the apostrophe and *s* (*'s*) are added to the last word of the phrase: the *University of Chicago's* second revolution in education, the *Bank of the Republic's* gold reserve.

5. To form the possessive plural of nouns, add an apostrophe if the plural ends in *s*: the *girls'* coats, *bankers'* hours.

6. If the plural does not end in *s*, add an apostrophe and *s* (*'s*): *children's* games, *women's* clubs.

7. To form the possessive plural of compound nouns, add an apostrophe and *s* (*'s*) at the end of the word: his *sons-in-law's* taxes.

8. In expressions like *someone else, everyone else, nobody else,* and *no one else,* add an apostrophe and *s* (*'s*) to *else: someone else's* car, *everyone else's* wishes, *no one else's* business, *nobody else's* responsibility.

9. To form the possessive of two or more words in a series connected by conjunctions and denoting joint possession, use the apostrophe and *s* (*'s*) after the last noun only: *Lord & Taylor's, Park and Tilford's.*

10. When joint possession is not denoted, use the apostrophe and *s* (*'s*) after each noun: *Macy's and Gimbel's, Altman's and Bonwit Teller's, Wordsworth's*

and Shelley's poetry, Kennedy's and Reagan's policies, ladies' and children's apparel.

11. In proper nouns ending in *s*, add an apostrophe and *s* (*'s*) to indicate the possessive: *Adams's* chronicle, *Dawes's* bank, *Cross's* theory, *Ayres's* references, *Ellis's* psychology, Sinclair *Lewis's* last novel, *Watkins's* lectures, Lily *Pons's* song recital, *Keats's* poems, *Dickens's* stories, *Brooks's* composition, Mrs. *Gates's* estate, *Wells's* History of the World, *Schultz's* case.

(1) Some authorities prefer to add only the apostrophe to nouns ending in *s* or an *s* sound; as, *Jones', Joneses', princes', princess', princesses'*, the *Schultzes* house.

(2) Notice the omission of apostrophes in some titles: *Teachers* College, *Governors* Island, *Citizens* Bank, American *Bankers* Association. But many organizations follow the general rule: The *Actors'* Dinner Club, Southern *Women's* Educational Alliance, *Veterans'* Administration.

12. The object of an action should be expressed by an *of-phrase* rather than by the possessive case: the assassination *of President Kennedy*, the retirement *of the Blakes*.

13. Note that the possessive case and the *of-phrase* may sometimes be used interchangeably, the choice often depending upon the sound of the expression in the sentence: the *secretary's* work or the work *of the secretary*, *Roosevelt's* Administration, or the Administration *of Roosevelt*. The possessive, however, does not always mean the same as the objective with the *of-phrase*. Compare *Mary's* picture, a picture *of Mary*.

14. In certain idiomatic expressions both the apostrophe and *s* (*'s*) and the *of-phrase* (sometimes called the double possessive) are used: This is a favorite pen *of John's*; I have examined that report *of the bookkeeper's*.

15. To denote the possessive of inanimate objects, an *of-phrase* is used instead of the possessive form: the

success *of that store,* the routine *of the office,* the chapters *of the book,* the thunder *of the surf.*

(1) When an inanimate object is personified, the apostrophe and *s* (*'s*) may be used: *Death's* approaching stride, *Love's* old sweet song.

(2) Certain idiomatic expressions referring particularly to time are writtten with the apostrophe and *s* (*'s*):

a day's vacation, a day's work, a day's journey, a week's work, a month's notice, four months' wages, a year's interest, three years' salary, but, *a two-year lease.* Notice also *a stone's throw, my heart's desire, the world's work, a dollar's worth, ten dollars' worth, thirty days' grace, the week's development.*

16. The *'s* may be added to figures, signs, symbols, and letters of the alphabet to form the plural. There is, however, a growing tendency to omit the apostrophe in such cases when there is no possibility of mistaking the meaning: *ABC's* or *ABCs, YMCA's* or *YMCAs.*

Your *a's* look very much like your *o's.*
In our great-grandmother's days the three *Rs* (or *R's*) formed the basis of education.
In the *1900s* (or *1900's*) technology spread through every aspect of human life, from transportation and cooking to *in vitro* fertilization.

17. Do not use an apostrophe to denote the omission of a letter or letters in an abbreviation.

Agcy.	chg.	pkg.	Supt.
Dept.	Comdt.	shpt.	Wm.
Chas.	pfd.	sgd.	mdse.

18. Sometimes the apostrophe is used in place of the first two figures for the year: the Class of '85, late in '79.

19. A noun modifying a gerund is usually in the possessive case.

I had not heard of *John's* leaving.
Perlman's playing of the *Kreutzer Sonata* delighted his audience.

20. For the use of the apostrophe in words referred to as nouns, *see* page 14.

Quotation Marks

1. Use double quotation marks to enclose a direct quotation.

"The force of a sentence may be measured to a great extent by the vigor of its verb," says Morton S. Freeman in *The Grammatical Lawyer*. "Verbs ignite the sparks that give life and movement to the sentence. And the power they generate far exceeds that of the most carefully selected noun or adjective."

"For the life of me, I can't understand why you want to learn to play the drum," declared her mother.

Do not use quotation marks to set off indirect questions.

Wrong: He remarked "that he was tired."
Right: He remarked that he was tired.
Right: He remarked, "I am tired."

Do not capitalize the first word of a quotation introduced indirectly in the text.

All my broker will say is that "it's just too early to spot a trend."

The Russian leader also cited what he called "the policy of boycotts, embargoes, 'punishments' and broken trade contracts that has become a habit with the United States."

Time

2. When two or more paragraphs are quoted, quotation marks should be placed at the beginning of each paragraph, but only at the end of the last.

"It is summer of the year I have spent at home in Oslo.
"I am sitting on a bench outside my house, eating home-made waffles and jam, forgetting that I want to lose weight. The heat is buzzing in my head.

"In Los Angeles no one would understand what it is like to have a feast of waffles in the sun after a long, dark winter. Life there is so remote from this."

LIV ULLMAN, *Changing*

Modern usage omits quotation marks around single extracts quoted in smaller type or placed in paragraphs indented on the left. Double spacing above and below the excerpt should be allowed to set it off from the rest of the text.

Robin Winks writes in *An American's Guide to Britain:*

One of the most common symbols on a highway map of Britain (and especially of England) is a tiny red mark that appears to have been lifted from the chess set; it indicates one of the several hundred castles, mostly in ruins, which dot the countryside. There may be other countries in which crenellated towers thrust from the landscape as often, but there can be no others in which so wide a variety of castle architecture is compressed in so small a space.

3. Use single quotation marks to enclose a quotation within a quotation. When it is necessary to use quotation marks within these, use double marks again.

We received the following instruction: "Proceed cautiously until you hear 'All clear' from the guard."
"When you learn to 'ankle' efficiently," said the cyclist, "you can ride for hours without tiring. 'Ankling' simply means efficient pedaling."

4. Use quotation marks or italics to set off from the context any quoted or emphasized word or short phrase.

With a "now-or-never" expression on his face, Bill marched into the manager's office.
One witness said the explosion lit up the predawn sky "like a doggone sunset."
The reporter asks "Who," "What," "Where," and "When." The interviewer also asks "Why."

5. Use quotation marks to enclose text following such terms as *entitled, the word, marked, designated, referred to as,* etc.

Following the word "can," insert "not."
All items marked "out" should be deleted.

But: Omit quotation marks after *so-called, known as,* and *called:*

Your so-called vacation home is actually rental property.
His son John, also known as Jack, is quite a golfer.

6. Quotation marks sometimes indicate the ironical use of words.

> Women may not have won equal rights yet, but they have "won" equal responsibilities.
>
> ELLEN GOODMAN, *At Large*

> Everyone in the dormitory "borrowed" my soap until it was all used up.

7. Quotation marks are used to enclose the titles of articles, poems, stories, speeches, and parts of whole printed works. The titles of periodicals, books, plays, operas, motion pictures, radio and television series, and other complete works are italicized.

> "Ruth Waltuch Jonas Opens Office in Norwalk"
> "Major Art Show in Washington"
> "Fighting to Cure the 'Incurable' "
> *The Nobel Prize Treasury* includes works by many famous authors.
> *Dallas* is seen weekly by millions of television fans.
> *A Prairie Home Companion* originates in Minneapolis.
> His first story appeared in *The New Yorker.*

Too many quotation marks on a page are unattractive. The titles of lectures, sermons, and the like on programs may be set in italic, small caps, or roman.

8. Following are rules for using quotation marks with other marks of punctuation:
   With the comma and the period, place quotation marks outside:

> "We shall always remember you," said the speaker, "as a dedicated leader, a cheerful giver, and a hopeless tennis player."

With the semicolon and the colon, quotation marks are placed inside:

The evidence looked, as Representative . . . would declare when it became public, "like a smoking gun"; it tied the President directly to a criminal obstruction of justice.

The New York Times

He gave up acting in westerns after many years of "tall in the saddle": he felt he had earned a change of scene.

With the exclamation point and the question mark, the quotation marks are placed outside when the quoted matter is an exclamation or a question:

"Look, Mommy, I'm flying!" cried the little boy.
"Can't you understand what I am saying?" she asked.

But: When the exclamation or question is not included, place the quotation marks inside:

Didn't you mean to say "deprecate" rather than "depreciate"?
I doubt that any mayor likes to be referred to in print as "hizzoner"!

With the dash, quotation marks are placed inside or outside the dash, depending on the context.

Suddenly—"Fire in the engine room!"—sounded through the dark.
She answered, "I suppose so, but—"

9. Use quotation marks around an unfamiliar word for the first use only.

A "bight" is formed by turning the rope end so that the end and the standing part (the rest of the rope) lie alongside each other. A square knot consists of two interwoven bights.

Fieldbook for Boys and Men (Boy Scouts of America)

10. Quotation marks should be omitted with such statements as:

I am writing to say thank you for all you have done.
We wish you all the best in the days ahead.

The Dash

1. Use a dash to indicate an abrupt change in a sentence.

> We see words that blow like leaves in the winds of autumn —golden words, bronze words, words that catch the light like opals.
>
> JAMES J. KILPATRICK, *The Writer's Art*

2. Sometimes a dash is used to set off interpolated explanatory matter.

> There are many differences—aside from the physical ones —between men and women.

> All through history young women have been to culture rather what wind is to thistledown—great carriers of it to new places.
>
> JOHN FOWLES, *The Enigma of Stonehenge*

3. Use a dash to indicate a sudden break in a sentence. (When a sentence ends in a dash, no period is needed.)

> "Let me know if you ever need—" She broke off in tears.
> I wouldn't—I couldn't permit you to say such a thing without a word of protest from me.

4. A dash may be used to set off a long phrase in apposition, particularly when the phrase is punctuated with commas.

> The male rampant—killing animals for food and clothing, digging out caves, and putting up huts, driving off enemies —early came to be associated in the mind of the elemental female with warmth, well-being, safety, and the kindred creature comforts.
>
> JAMES THURBER, "Listen to This, Dear"

> We also increase value by providing more options—a wider range of choice.

5. A pair of dashes may be used instead of parentheses.

> All branches of the family produced their individual eccentrics—there was even an uncle who believed in the Single

Tax—but they were united in their solid understanding of the value of money as the basis of a firm stance in this world.

KATHARINE ANNE PORTER, "Gertrude Stein: A Self-Portrait"

It is obvious that practitioners of opera—especially in our age when the trend toward cultivation of the languages in which operas were originally written is strong—must know other languages in addition to their own mother tongue.

ERICH LEINSDORF, *The Composer's Advocate*

6. Use a dash instead of the word *to* in reference to dates, pages, paragraphs, verses, and cantos.

1910–1940	Genesis 2:10–14
pages 10–49	verses 5–10
paragraphs 1–14	Cantos I–IV

7. Use a series of dashes under names in a catalogue to indicate repetition.

Crow, John A.   *Italy: A Journey Through Time*
——.   *Mexico Today*
——.   *Spain: The Root and the Flower*

But note that the dash for this purpose must never be used at the top of a page.

Parentheses

1. Use parentheses to set off parenthetical matter not necessary to the grammatical structure of the sentence but too important to omit. (Shorter expressions of this kind may be set off by commas or dashes.)

People who are constantly expecting disaster (and I count myself among them) can always produce examples of such events to prove their point.

The due date of the monthly payment (once the loan has been approved) can be the day most convenient for you.

[Evelyn Waugh] too took great quantities of Latin (and Greek as well), and recalled in his autobiography that he forgot all of it as he grew older.

JAMES J. KILPATRICK, *The Writer's Art*

2. Parentheses may be used to enclose figures or letters marking the divisions of a subject.

The search for a new executive director involved:
(a) Placing advertisements in professional journals and newspapers in the area
(b) Evaluating the résumés received and choosing the ten most promising for interviews
(c) Interviewing the ten finalists

We set our priorities as follows:
(1) To raise funds to meet our present budget
(2) To provide an endowment for future funding
(3) To seek a larger building for the agency

Parentheses are omitted when using Roman numerals.

3. Use parentheses to enclose explanations inserted in the text.

The Oyster Festival (a recently established event) has become a popular celebration in Norwalk.
The figure of a knight in armor (see plate 4) shows the style worn by King Richard I.
Use spring water only. (Chlorinated water will darken the color in the final stages.)

4. In legal documents or whenever double form is required, use parentheses to enclose a figure inserted to confirm a statement given in words: thirty (30) days; sixty (60) dollars, *not* sixty dollars (60); twenty dollars ($20), *not* twenty ($20) dollars.

5. The use of parentheses with other marks of punctuation requires careful consideration. No additional punctuation is needed with parentheses unless it is needed to clarify the meaning of the sentence.
With the period outside:

Among those mentioned in the article on pianists was Willie "The Lion" Smith (1897–1973).
Take the blue-blazed trail down a moderately steep slope to the inlet of Riga Lake (3.5 miles).

With the period inside:

The value of the stolen jewelry was not mentioned. (It later developed that the jewelry had not been appraised for many years.)
If copy reads 3½ million dollars, change to read $3.5 million. (To be used only in amounts of a million or more.)

With the question mark and the exclamation point:

Mr. McLean (or was it Mr. McLune?) asked to be remembered to you.
Will you please call the concierge (or whatever he calls himself)?
Walking is a highly recommended exercise (and I don't mean strolling!).
Thomas Jefferson sold his library of 6,000 volumes for $23,950 (less than half its auction value)!

Note: The exclamation point or question mark, enclosed in parentheses, is sometimes used to express irony or sarcasm.

The effect of his oration (?) was to induce sleep in his audience rather than to arouse us to action.
A recent graduate of a leading college wrote that he was *elegeble* (!) and interested in obtaining a *franchize* (!).

Do not use a comma, semicolon, or colon in front of an opening parenthesis.

Right: He lives in Minot (N.D.) and attends college in Chicago.
Wrong: He lives in Minot, (N.D.) and attends college in Chicago.
Right: This case (124 U.S. 329) is not relevant.
Wrong: This case, (124 U.S. 329) is not relevant.

Do not place a comma, semicolon, or colon after the closing parenthesis unless such punctuation would be needed if there were no parentheses.

When we arrived, we found a young man (presumably the fiancé) talking to Jenny's mother.
Interviews will be held next week for freshmen (Tues., 10–12 A.M.); sophomores (Wed., 2–4 P.M.); juniors (Thurs., 10–12 A.M.); and seniors (Thurs., 2–4 P.M.).

Brackets

1. Use brackets to enclose words and phrases independent of the sentence, such as explanatory notes, omissions, and comments that are not written by the author of the text.

The following year [1620] the Pilgrims landed at Plymouth.

[Marshall] still retains that vigor of intellect which has for so many years rendered him the ornament of the bench.

HUGH GRIGSBY, quoted in *John Marshall* by LEONARD BAKER

2. Use brackets to enclose *sic* following an error in spelling or usage in copied matter.

The Rosevelt [*sic*] family contibuted two presidents.
Be sure to buy Hawaiin [*sic*] pineapples.

3. No punctuation is used with brackets unless required by the matter bracketed and the sense of the rest of the sentence.

Between human beings [Galbraith wrote] there is a type of intercourse which proceeds not from knowledge, or even from lack of knowledge, but from failure to know what isn't known.

JOHN KENNETH GALBRAITH, *The Great Crash 1929*

No punctuation is used before or after bracketed matter inserted in a quotation.

Ellipsis Dots

Ellipsis is the term for omission of words or paragraphs from a quotation. It is indicated by the use of period dots. Within a sentence, the dots follow any punctuation in the quotation. A space is left before each dot and also after the last if a word follows.

Cézanne's world is still to the point of being timeless. The landscapes, while they often give a vivid sense of reality, are rarely seen at a particular time of day or in particular light conditions, . . . but rather in a situation as permanent as if they had been represented by a sense of touch rather than by sight.

JAMES S. ACKERMAN, *Brief Lives*

There are other countries, as well as Greece as it now is, where it is possible to learn important elements of the ancient world. . . . One can study the permutations of Greek architecture all over Europe, and see the most thrilling Greek museum material all over America. But the country itself, with its special climate, its own sea, its unique limestone and marble geography, and above all its language and its ruins, still has something special to say, something genuine, something not said elsewhere.

PETER LEVI in *The Greek World* by Eliot Porter

When a paragraph or more of text is omitted within a quotation, a line of spaced periods is used to indicate the ellipsis. The periods are spaced apart; three, five, or seven are used, depending on the width of the page.

Hyphenation and Compounds

The Hyphen: General Uses

A hyphen is used to indicate the following:

(1) Words compounded of two or more words to represent a single idea.

(2) The division of a word into syllables.

(3) The division of a word at the end of a line.

Since usage varies, it is impossible to make inflexible rules for hyphenating phrases. Two or more words which represent a single idea may stand as separate words or become hyphenated or be written as one word. The usual sequence is for the words to be written separate at first, then to become hyphenated, and finally to be written solid. The overall rule is to avoid ambiguity.

When there is doubt whether a phrase should be written solid, as two words, or hyphenated, it is advisable to consult an authoritative source, such as an up-to-date dictionary.

The following rules may be regarded as a guide to current practice.

1. Use a hyphen as follows between units forming a compound adjective before the noun modified:

first-class bond
deep-blue color
four-year-old girl
house-to-house search
one- and two-story houses
a medium-sized
   commercial town
long-distance telephone

one-man job
up-to-date fashion
high-minded attitude
hard-hitting policy
teacher-pupil
   relationship
Three-State Bus Line

Note that the hyphen should be inserted after a series of hyphenated adjectives modifying the same noun when the noun occurs after the last adjective only: *four-, five-, and six-story buildings; 7- to 10-day trips; 29-year-old bird.*

2. When a compound adjective follows the noun or the predicate, ordinarily it is not hyphenated.

Many fashions, popular and up to date, will be on display.
His fame, well deserved and worldwide, rests on his scientific achievements.

3. An adverb ending in *ly* is not joined with a hyphen to the adjective that it qualifies; as, a *highly* developed intelligence, a *fully* balanced ration, a *beautifully* told story.

4. Surnames written with a hyphen are in most cases considered as one name; as, Harley *Granville-Barker,* Sheila *Kaye-Smith,* and Madame *Schumann-Heink.*

5. Proper names used adjectively are not joined by a hyphen; as, *New England* winters, *Fifth Avenue* shoppers, *South American* Indians.
   But notice such forms as *German-American, Anglo-Indian, Indo-European,* which are purely adjective in nature and always hyphenated.

6. Use a hyphen in compound numerals; as, *forty-six,* *twenty-one* hundredths, *twenty-first.*

7. Use a hyphen when compounding numerals with other words; as, *five-o'clock* tea, *twenty-foot* pole, *150-yard* dash.

8. Fractions are hyphenated when the word is used as an adjective; as, They are entitled to *ten and one-half* shares of stock. When the fraction is used as a noun no hyphen is necessary; as, He invested *one third* of his money in real estate. But there is a growing tendency in business writing to use the hyphen in both the adjective and the noun.

9. Use a hyphen in certain compounds made up of nouns and prepositional phrases.

sons-in-law	hand-to-hand	fleur-de-lis
man-of-war	straight-from-the-shoulder	vis-à-vis

However, there are many exceptions to this rule: *commander in chief, editor in chief, maître d'hôtel,* and many others.

10. Use a hyphen in titles compounded with *ex* and *elect*.

ex-Governor	Governor-elect
ex-Senator	President-elect
ex-President	Vice President-elect

11. Civil and military titles (single) are not hyphenated.

GPO Style Manual

Civil Titles

Ambassador at Large	Chief of Police
Ambassador Extraordinary and Plenipotentiary	Chief of Protocol
Assistant Secretary	Congressman at Large
Associate Justice	Consul General
Attorney at Law	Counselor of Embassy
Attorney General	Deputy Commissioner
Chargé d'Affaires	Director General
Chief Clerk	Editor in Chief
Chief Executive	Envoy Extraordinary and
Chief Justice	Minister
Chief Magistrate	Plenipotentiary
	First Secretary

Second Secretary
Third Secretary
Governor General
Inspector General
Lieutenant Governor
Military Attaché
Naval Attaché
Naval Attaché
Postmaster General

Public Printer
Secretary of Labor
Secretary General of the
  United Nations
Sergeant at Arms
Under Secretary
Vice Consul
Vice President

Words denoting the office itself are hyphenated; as *under-secretaryship, vice-presidency.*

Military and Naval Titles

Adjutant General
Brigadier General
Brigadier General
  Commandant
Commander in Chief
Lieutenant Colonel
Lieutenant Commander

Lieutenant General
Major General
Quartermaster General
Rear Admiral
Surgeon General
Vice Admiral

In British usage the following titles are hyphenated:

Field-Marshal
Lieutenant-Colonel
Lieutenant-Commander
Lieutenant-General

Major-General
Rear-Admiral
Vice-Admiral

12. Use the hyphen in compounds made up of prefixes joined to proper names.

anti-American
mid-Atlantic
mid-August
neo-Platonism
pan-Hellenic

pseudo-Gothic
un-American
anti-suffragist
non-European
Pan-American

For capitalizing words in titles and headings that form parts of hyphenated compounds, *see* pp. 73–74.

13. Do not ordinarily use the hyphen between a prefix and the stem when the added word is not a proper noun.

antisocial	intramural
biannual	nonconformist
bicentennial	nonessential
biennial	nonofficial
coauthor	preview
extracurricular	retroactive
foreclose	semiyearly
intercollegiate	supermarket

Compounds are hyphenated when otherwise a vowel would be confusingly doubled in combination: *anti-imperialist, co-owner, intra-atomic, semi-independent.*

Exceptions: *Cooperate* and *coordinate* and their derivatives are usually written thus as solid forms, because of their great frequency and familiarity.

14. Use the hyphen in the following examples to distinguish words spelled alike but differing in meaning:

re-cover, to cover again	re-count, to count again
recover, to regain	recount, to relate in detail

15. Use the hyphen to form adjectives compounded with *well* preceding the noun; as, *well-bred, well-born, well-to-do, well-earned, well-expressed, well-known.*

His *well-known* courtesy made him a favorite.

Do not use the hyphen with such expressions when they follow the word modified.

She showed herself a woman *well versed* in the ways of the world.

16. Use the hyphen generally in words compounded with *self* as a prefix; as, *self-conceit, self-confidence, self-control, self-reliance, self-respect, self-starter, self-assured, self-explaining, self-governing, self-made, self-taught, self-willed.*

Do not use the hyphen in *selfsame* and *selfless* or in pronouns compounded with *self;* as, *myself, himself, herself, itself, oneself, ourselves, themselves.*

17. Foreign phrases used adjectively should not be hyphenated; as, an *a priori* argument, a *noblesse oblige* attitude, an *ex cathedra* pronouncement.

Guide to Compounding

In the following list, forms marked (G) are written in accordance with the *GPO Style Manual,* those marked (W) are in accordance with *Webster's Ninth New Collegiate Dictionary,* those not marked are in accordance with both books.

aforementioned
afterthought
airbase (G)
air base (W)
airbrake (G)
air brake (W)
airfield
airline
airmail
airplane
airport
all right
anybody
anyhow
any one (of them)
anyone (anybody)
anything
audiofrequency
audiovisual
bankbook
banknote (G)
bank note (W)
basketball
bas-relief
beforehand
billboard
birthrate
blood bank
blood count
blood poisoning
blood pressure

blood test
blood type
blood vessel
blueprint
boathouse
bodyguard
bombproof
bombshell
bondholder
bond paper
bookbinding
bookcase
book review
bookshop
boxcar
box office
box spring
briefcase
broadcaster
businesslike
businessman
bylaws
byline
byproduct (G)
by-product (W)
cardboard
carport
cash account
cashbook
cash register
chain letter

chainstore (G)
chain store (W)
checkbook
chinaware
choirboy
clapboard
classmate
classroom
clearinghouse
closeup (G)
close-up (W)
clubroom
coauthor
coeducation
coffee shop
committeeman
common sense (noun)
commonsense (adj.)
countdown
court-martial
courtroom
crosscurrent
cross-examination
cross-fertilize
cross-pollinate
cross-purpose
cross-reference
cross section
crossword
dateline
daybook
day letter
dining room
double entry
dry goods
east-northeast
en route
everybody
everywhere
ex officio
extracurricular
extra dividend
fairway

filmstrip
fireproof
first aid
flagstaff
foolproof
footnote
forthcoming
free trade
free will (noun)
galley proof
good will (kindness) (G)
goodwill (asset) (G)
goodwill (both) (W)
handwriting
headline
high frequency
horsepower
house organ
inasmuch
insofar
job lot
landowner
lawbreaker
layoff
letterhead
living room
loudspeaker
makeup
markdown (noun)
mark down (verb) (W)
midsummer
money order
moreover
network
nevertheless
newscaster
newsreel
night letter
noonday
northwest
notebook
note paper
notwithstanding

office boy
officeholder
offset
packinghouse
paperback
papercutter (G)
paper cutter (W)
parcel post
passbook
paymaster
payroll
per annum
percent
policyholder
postcard
postmark
postmaster
post office
racecourse
salesclerk
sales tax
school board
schoolhouse
shopwindow
signpost
stockbroker
stock exchange
stock market
stockpile
stopgap

subcommittee
subdivision
taxpayer
textbook
thereafter
time clock
timekeeper
timesaving
timetable
titleholder
title page
toastmaster
toll road
trademark
trade name
transatlantic
transcontinental
turnover
viewpoint
violet ray
wage earner
wavelength
wax paper
waybill
weekend
workday
X-ray (verb)
X ray (noun)
yearbook

Division of Words

Avoid all unnecessary divisions. Pronunciation is usually the best guide in determining how to divide words into syllables. An important principle to follow is that the part of the word left at the end of the line should suggest the part beginning the next line.

1. Do not divide monosyllables: *friend, through, stopped.*

2. Divide words of two syllables at the end of the first: *pave-ment, Eng-lish.*

3. Do not divide words of four letters or, if avoidable, those of five or six: *item, index, supper, needed.*

4. Do not divide a word on a single letter or on two letters: *able,* not *a-ble; omit,* not *o-mit; ratio,* not *rati-o,* or *ra-tio; only,* not *on-ly.*

5. In words beginning with prefixes, divide, if possible, on the prefix: *mis-pronounce, sub-sidize.*

6. Never let more than two consecutive lines end with a hyphen if it can be avoided.

7. Do not divide such suffixes as the following:

cial	*in*	spe-cial
tial		pala-tial
cion		coer-cion
sion		occa-sion
tion		administra-tion
cious		falla-cious
geous		gor-geous
gious		conta-gious
tious		frac-tious

8. Separate suffixes, as a rule, from the stem of the word: *hop-ing, dear-est.*

9. In general, the following endings make reasonable divisions: *able, ance, ant, ence, ent, ible, ical, tive.*

accept-ance	prefer-ence
account-ant	correspond-ent
consider-able	crea-tive

10. In general, divide a word between double consonants unless the stem *ends* in a double consonant.

embar-rass	*but*	assess-ment
forgot-ten		bill-ing
mil-lion		full-est
neces-sary		odd-ity
occur-rence		pass-able
refer-ring		profess-ing
win-ning		tell-ing

11. Words containing a single middle consonant are divided as follows:

    (a) If the preceding vowel is short and the syllable accented, let the consonant end the syllable: *balance, pun-ish.*
    (b) If the preceding vowel is long, write the consonant with the following syllable: *le-gal, oppo-nent.*

12. Solid compounds should usually be divided between the members: *book-keeper, care-taker, date-line, forth-coming, type-write.*

13. When a hyphenated compound must be divided at the end of a line, divide on the hyphen: *forty-five, law-abiding, long-distance.*

14. Unless absolutely necessary, do not divide names of persons or other proper nouns.

15. Do not separate such titles as *Capt., Dr., Esq., Mr., Mrs., Rev., St.,* or abbreviations for degrees, from names to which they belong.

16. Do not separate abbreviations for societies, radio stations, and the like: *YWCA, WBDO.*

17. Do not separate initials preceding a name.

18. Do not divide a word at the end of a page or paragraph if it is possible to avoid doing so.

19. Do not add another hyphen to words already hyphenated: not *self-con-trol,* but *self-control.*

20. When two vowels come together but are sounded separately, divide them into separate syllables: *genealogy, cre-ation.*

Use of Italics

1. Italics are often used to give emphasis to words or expressions. They should be used only for strong emphasis, never indiscriminately. To indicate italics, underline in manuscript the words to be so printed.

I know you can't spend *all* your time comparing grammatical authorities.

When one writes that a job requries ten *man-hours,* one should be aware that a large number of readers will perceive the term as a sexist slur.

2. Italicize all punctuation immediately following italicized words.

3. Italicize the words *Continued, To be continued, Continued on page,* and *To be concluded.*

4. Italicize the words, *See also, See* before a cross-reference in an index; also the words *For* and *read* in a list of errata placed at the beginning or at the end of a volume.

   See also legumes.
   For Rosevelt *read* Roosevelt.

5. Abbreviations of Latin words in common use are not usually italicized; as, e.g., etc., i.e., c. (ca. or circ.), viz., and vs. However, it is preferable not to abbreviate *versus,* as in "Yale versus Harvard" except in informal writing. For the use of *v.* in legal references, *see* pages 121–22.

6. Italicize the following Latin abbreviations, words, and phrases used in literary and legal references:

ad loc. (to the place)	*op. cit.* (work cited)
et al. (and others)	*passim* (here and there)
et seq. (and the following)	*sc.* (namely)
fl. (lived)	*sic* (thus)
ibid. (the same reference)	*s.v.* (under a word or
idem (the same place)	heading)
infra (below)	*vide* (see)
loc. cit. (place cited)	

7. Use italics when a word is spoken of as a word. (*See also* p. 103.)

   The word *gay* now carries a different connotation from its meaning in Cornelia Otis Skinner's *Our Hearts Were Young and Gay.*

8. Foreign words and phrases not yet adopted into English should be underlined in letters and manuscripts and italicized in printed matter.

Current Merriam-Webster dictionaries (*Webster's Third New International* and the *Ninth New Collegiate*) do not indicate, as did earlier editions, foreign words and phrases that may not yet be anglicized. In *The Random House Dictionary of the English Language*, the editors have distinguished between words and phrases considered to be anglicized and those considered to remain foreign by printing the latter in italic type. The following list of words and phrases are printed in roman type in *The Random House Dictionary*, indicating that they are anglicized and need *not* be underlined or marked for italics:

addendum	communiqué	hors d'oeuvre
ad hoc	confrere	in memoriam
ad infinitum	contretemps	levee
ad interim	coup	maître d'hôtel
agenda	coup d'état	mandamus
à la carte	cul-de-sac	matériel
à la mode	debris	mélange
ante-bellum	décolleté	melee
ante meridiem	denouement	ménage
a priori	détente	morale
apropos	dilettante	mores
artiste	distrait	naïve, naïveté
attaché	dramatis personae	noblesse oblige
beau ideal	éclat	nom de plume
belles-lettres	elite	opus
billet-doux	en route	papier-mâché
blasé	ensemble	penchant
bloc	entente	per annum
bona fide	entourage	per capita
cabaret	entree	per contra
camouflage	entrepreneur	per diem
canapé	ex officio	porte-cochere
carte blanche	exposé	poseur
chargé d'affaires	fete	post meridiem
chef-d'oeuvre	habeas corpus	post-mortem
cliché	habitué	précis

prima facie	regime	tête-à-tête
procès-verbal	reveille	tour de force
pro rata	résumé	vice versa
protégé	soiree	visa
quasi	status quo	vis-à-vis
quondam	subpoena	viva voce
recherché	table d'hôte	

Note that in spelling many of these once-foreign words and phrases, the accent marks used in the original language are retained in English.

9. Italics are used for the titles of long poems, works of art, long musical compositions, books, magazines, newspapers, pamphlets, plays, motion pictures, and radio and television series. *But:* The title of an episode in a television series is set in roman and enclosed in quotation marks.

El amor brujo	the *Birmingham Post-*
At Dawn We Slept	*Herald*
Popular Photography	the *Mona Lisa*
Arizona Highways	*Romeo and Juliet*
Dynasty	*All Things Considered*
Inside the Financial	*The Mystery of Edwin*
Futures Market	*Drood*

The names of songs and short musical compositions, short stories and subdivisions of books, and magazine or newspaper articles are not italicized. They are set in roman and enclosed in quotation marks. (*See* page 102.)

10. The names of ships, trains, aircraft, and spacecraft are italicized. However, the type of plane is not.

the M.S. *Nederland*	the shuttle *Columbia*
the *Washingtonian*	DC 10
the carrier *Ticonderoga*	Boeing 747

11. Legal usage italicizes all case names, including the "v.," and any procedural phrases in text of briefs, articles, books, etc., but never in footnotes.

Mapp v. Ohio
Elkins v. United States
In re Sumner
Ex parte John Chase
Lehman v. City of Shaker Heights
Ortega y Gasset v. Feliciano Santiago

The above examples are from *A Uniform System of Citation,* published by The Harvard Law Review Association, Cambridge, Mass. For more detailed rules for legal usage, see that comprehensive manual. In a non-legal context, italics are not used; as, the Sumner case.

The *GPO Style Manual* rules differ in some details.

The local legal printers will know the form preferred by a local court as to printed briefs. But consult local rules for the specific color required for brief covers.

12. Italicize the binomial (scientific) names of genera and species.

   Salix babylonica, Acer rubrum, Sinningia speciosa

   Do not italicize the names of genera without the species, or of groups of higher rank (classes, orders, families, tribes, etc.); as, the family Leguminosae.

13. Italicize *Resolved* in resolutions and legislative acts, as well as *Provided* when used in the body of this matter.

   Resolved, That the President shall be authorized to represent this body at the convention to be held . . .
   Resolved by the Common Council of the City of Norwalk, That the sum of $40,000 be designated for the purchase of . . . : *Provided,* That . . .

14. In preparing matter for publication, use italics for a title following a signature: Stephen G. Albert, *Treasurer.*

15. Do not use italics for foreign titles or designations of foreign leaders; as, Emir, Principessa; or for names of foreign legislatures or institutions; as, the British House of Commons, the Riksdag, the Pinakothek, the Museo Napoleonico, Akershus Fortress.

CHAPTER SIX

Expressing Numbers

In general, the question of expressing a number in words or in figures is decided in terms of clarity and formality. In formal or semiformal writing, the tendency is to use words, while in business communications and popular magazines, figures are often used for easy comprehension.

Book

> The Teatro Puerto Rico has a concert hall of thirteen hundred seats and two movie theaters of three hundred seats each.

Letter

> The Teatro Puerto Rico has a concert hall of 1,300 seats and two movie theaters of 300 seats each.

1. ROUND NUMBERS

Spell out all round numbers and approximate amounts; as, *four or five feet, seven hundred miles, a thousand reasons, almost a million board feet of lumber, a man in his eighties.*

When round numbers greater than one thousand are spelled out, such as 1,850, use *eighteen hundred and fifty* or *one thousand eight hundred and fifty.*

The word *and* may or may not be used between tens and units. Modern usage seems to prefer omitting it; as, *three hundred five.*

Spell out round sums of money if the amount can be expressed in one or two words; as, *forty-five dollars, two hundred dollars, seven thousand dollars.* Use the dollar sign and spell out *million* and *billion* to express large

124

amounts in even millions or tenths of millions; as, *$1.5 million, $8.7 million, between $10 and $20 million.*

2. NUMBERS AT BEGINNING OF SENTENCE

Spell out all numbers at the beginning of a sentence, even when other numbers in the sentence are expressed in figures.

> Two carloads of new, sample-grade corn were received here today and sold at 85 to 99 cents a bushel.
> Twenty members were present at last month's meeting.

When a long number begins a sentence, change the wording so that the number appears later.

> *Not:* 1,625 pairs of shoes were destroyed in the fire.
> *Better:* The fire destroyed 1,625 pairs of shoes.
> *Not:* 135 employees will retire this year.
> *Better:* This year 135 employees will retire.

3. NUMBERS WITHIN A SENTENCE

Spell out numbers from one through ten, except in a series of related numbers.

> The two boys consumed 4 hamburgers, 2 cans of soda, and 6 cookies.
> The football team won 8 games and lost 2 last year.

In formal writing, numbers that can be expressed in one or two words are spelled out, but figures may be used in letters or reports.

> It is estimated that there may be up to thirty-nine bankruptcies per thousand businesses in this area. (Text of a book)
> The subsurface formation ranges between depths of 3 and 34 feet from the ground surface. (Text of a report)

Use figures to express definite amounts and longer numbers.

> The hotel received the record number of 3,138 requests for reservations this year.
> His house was sold for $91,500.

This month 1,977,639 shares were traded, compared with
2,320,003 last month.
The foundation unit cost per square foot varies from $15.50
to $88.30, depending on the building weight per square
foot.

Related numbers or amounts within a sentence should
be expressed entirely in figures or entirely in words unless
doing so would cause confusion.

They employed 10 women for 3 weeks at $200 a week. *Or:*
They employed ten women for three weeks at two hundred
dollars a week.

Avoid placing next to each other two numbers referring
to different things:

Wrong: In 1981 15 states ratified the law.
Right: In 1981 fifteen states ratified the law.
Allowed: In 1981, 15 states ratified the law.
Wrong: 2 3-bedroom apartments, 3 $2 bets
Right: two 3-bedroom apartments, three $2 bets

When one number immediately precedes another, spell
out one, preferably the one with the fewer letters; as, *ten
3-inch nails, 20 six-foot poles.*

4. DATES

In decades and centuries: Spell out numbers referring
to decades and centuries; as, the *gay nineties,* the *nineteenth century.*

In years: In social correspondence, as in wedding invitations, express years in words, as *nineteen hundred and
sixty-nine;* but in formal and legal documents, write *one
thousand nine hundred and sixty-nine.*

In letters: Use figures, as a general rule, in the heading
of a business letter to express the date; as, *January 27,
1986, not 1/27/86* or *January 27th, 1986.*

In European usage and in military practice, the day
precedes the month in letter headings; as, *2 May, 1986.*

In the body of a business letter, when the name of the
month precedes the date, the date should be written in
figures without *-st, -d,* or *-th.*

Make the appointment for January 22. (*Not:* January twenty-second or January 22d.)

When the name of the month follows the date or when the name of the month is omitted, the date should be written in full or in figures with the ordinal abbreviation.

Make the appointment for the twenty-second of January *or* the twenty-second *or* the 22d of January *or* the 22d. (*Not:* the 22 of January *or* the 22.)

Our representative will be in Boston on November 19, 20, and 21. Would it be convenient for you to see him on the 20th or the 21st?

Note the acceptable methods of writing dates:

May 1977 *or* May, 1977   May 25, 1977 (*not:* May 25th, 1977
June 6 to July 15, 1977 (*not:* June 6, 1977 to July 15, 1977.)
April, May, and June, 1987 (*but:* May and June 1987 *or* May and June, 1987)

When abbreviating decades or dates, in informal writing, use an apostrophe to indicate the omission; as *the Class of '68.*

In referring to a fiscal year, consecutive years, or a continuous period of two years or more, when contracted, the forms used are 1906–38, 1961–62, 1801–2, 1875–79 (*but:* 1895–1914, 1900–1901). For two or more separate years not representing a continuous period, a comma is used instead of a dash (1945, 1949). If the word *from* precedes the year or the word *inclusive* follows it, the second year is not shortened and the word *to* is used instead of the dash; as, *from 1983 to 1986; 1985 to 1986, inclusive.*

In dates, A.D. precedes the year (A.D. 937); B.C. follows the year (254 B.C.).

In formal invitations, announcements, and acceptances, dates are invariably spelled out; as, *February Twenty-first, Nineteen Hundred and Sixty-nine,* or *February Twenty First, Nineteen Hundred and Sixty Nine.*

In legal documents, such as wills and deeds, dates are

invariably written out; as, *the twelfth day of January, one thousand nine hundred and eighty-four.*

5. TIME OF DAY

Spell out the time of day in text matter.
(1) Use *a.m., p.m.* or A.M., P.M., in connection with figures; as,

1:30 a.m.	1:30 p.m.	1:30 A.M.

Note that when the time is spelled out, the abbreviations a.m. or p.m. must not be used:

> The train left at three in the afternoon.
> *Not:* The train left at three p.m.

(2) Add zeroes to the even hour only if a time containing minutes appears in the same sentence.

> He will be on duty from 8:00 a.m. to 4:30 p.m.

6. STREETS

In the text spell out numbers of streets, avenues, wards, and districts; as, *Forty-second Street, Sixth Avenue, Thirteenth District, Ninth Ward.*

In writing streets and avenues, spell out the names of those up to twelve; as, *Fifth Avenue, Ninth Street.*

In correspondence express numbers above twelve in figures; as *121 Street* or *121st Street.*

7. PAGE NUMBERS

Use figures for page numbers; as, page 3, page 533.

8. REFERENCES IN FOOTNOTES

In footnotes and in all bibliographical material, abbreviate a word designating a part when followed by a number.

Chap. III	col. 2 (cols.)
Vol. II (pl. Vols.)	art. 14 (arts.)
Fig. 80 (Figs.)	p. 1 (pp.)
sec. 3 (secs.)	pp. 6f. (page 6 and the
No. 1 (Nos.)	following page)

pp. 6ff. (page 6 and the following pages)	pp. 5–8 (pages 5 to 8 inclusive)

Section is usually abbreviated in enumeration, except the first:

Section 1
Sec.   2
Sec.   3

In legal work, *Section* and *Sections* are abbreviated by the use of the symbols § and §§, respectively.

9. SUMS OF MONEY

For typographical appearance and easy grasp of large numbers, beginning with million, the word million or billion is used:

12 million (*not* 12,000,000); 12 billion
$2,750 million (*not* $2,750,000,000)
two and a half million dollars (*not* $2½ million)
300,000 (*not* 300 thousand)
amounting to 4 millions
5 or 10 billion dollars' worth

(1) In bills and in other distinctly financial statements, the symbol for cents is used when given in cents only; as, *steers low, 25¢ to 40¢ lower.*

(2) Do not use both figures and words for sums of money except in commercial and legal documents. When both are used, parentheses follow the completed expression; as, thirty dollars ($30) or thirty (30) dollars, *not* thirty ($30) dollars. The custom of using both figures and words for sums of money is seldom used today in letters.

10. DECIMALS

Use figures for expressing decimals and percentages, but spell out percentages when they begin a sentence.

0.832; 10.5
The Saskatchewan official reports said 80 percent of the wheat in that province had been threshed.
Ten percent will be the profit.

In writing a decimal fraction not preceded by a whole number, a zero is placed before it except when the decimal begins with a zero; as, 0.235, .0235.

In letters and formal writing, the word *percent* should be used instead of the symbol %. In commercial work, such as tabular matter, the symbol % is used.

11. FRACTIONS

Fractions standing alone or expressed in a single compound word are usually written out; as, *half* a mile, a *quarter* of an ounce, a *one-third* interest.

Fractions should be expressed in words or as decimals where possible; as, 20.5 miles, *not* 20 and a half miles *or* 20½ miles.

Written-out fractions used as adjectives must be hyphenated; as, a *two-thirds* vote, *one-half* inch; but when they are used as nouns, they are usually not hyphenated; as, *one sixth* of the estate, *two fifths* of the field. In business writing there is a growing tendency to use the hyphen for both the adjective and the noun; as, a *one-third* interest in the estate, *one-third* of the estate.

In general, a fraction expressed in figures should not be followed by *of a, of an.*

⅜ inch, *not* ⅜ of an inch   ⅔ cup, *not* ⅔ of a cup
0.5 percent, *not* ½ of 1 percent

It is incorrect to use *nd, th,* and *ths* after fractions:

⁶⁄₁₀₀, *not* ⁶⁄₁₀₀ths   ⁴⁄₁,₀₀₀, *not* ⁴⁄₁,₀₀₀ths
¹⁄₃₂, *not* ¹⁄₃₂nd part   ¹⁄₁₆, *not* ¹⁄₁₆th
Better: .06 inch, .004

Mixed numbers, when expressed in figures, should be typed with a space rather than a hyphen between the integer and the fraction; as, 23 3/4, *not* 23-3/4.

When fractions are used in giving specifications, the hyphen is used and the noun is always singular:

a 4½-inch pipe   a 1¼-inch belt   a .22-caliber rifle

When a fraction is the subject of a sentence, the verb agrees with the noun in the prepositional phrase.

Two thirds of his income *is* from real estate.
Two thirds of their incomes *are* from real estate.

With *one* as subject followed by a fraction, the verb is singular.

One and five-sixth yards is enough.
One and a half teaspoonfuls was the usual dosage.

12. AGES

In stating definite ages, usage differs. In general, figures should be used for ready comprehension; as, My age is 52 years, 6 months, 10 days; a boy 6 years old; 3-year-old colt; 2-month-old child.

In formal writing or when the age is indefinite, references to ages should be spelled out; as, eighty years and four months old; children between six and fourteen; a man in his forties.

13. RESULTS OF BALLOTS

These should be expressed by figures; as, 38 for, 25 against; yeas 56, nays 24.

14. DIMENSIONS

In text, to represent dimensions write 10 by 15 inches, *not* 10 x 15 inches *or* 10″ x 15″.

In technical work, use ′ for feet, ″ for inches, and x for *by:* 9′ x 11″. In ordinary writing, abbreviate but do not capitalize dimensions; as, 6 ft. 11 in.

15. DISTANCES

Write in figures all measures of distances except a fraction of a mile; as, 16 miles, 12 yards, 3 feet; *but* one-half mile.

16. MEASURES

Enumerations of measure must be expressed by figures; as, 10 gallons, 4 quarts, and 3 pints; 60 bushels, 5 pecks. In ordinary writing, they are abbreviated; as, 6 lbs. 3 oz.

17. TEMPERATURE

Use figures followed by degree sign and the abbreviation *F.* for Fahrenheit or *C.* for Celsius; as, 32°F., 45°C.

18. WEIGHTS

Enumeration of weight should be expressed in figures; as, 2 tons, 40 pounds, 10 ounces.

19. METRIC SYSTEM

Abbreviate after a numeral all designations of weights and measures in the metric system. The period may be omitted, according to the National Bureau of Standards.

20. ROMAN NUMERALS

The following table represents Roman numerals commonly used:

1—I	6—VI	11—XI
2—II	7—VII	14—XIV
3–III	8—VIII	18—XVIII
4—IV or IIII	9—IX	19—XIX
5—V	10—X	20—XX

30—XXX	300—CCC	2,000—MM
40—XL	400—CCCC or	3,000—MMM
50—L	CD	4,000—M$\bar{\text{V}}$
60—LX	500—D	5,000—$\bar{\text{V}}$
70—LXX	600—DC	1928—
80—LXXX	700—DCC	MCMXXVIII
90—XC	800—DCCC	1930—
100—C	900—CM	MCMXXX
200—CC	1,000—M	1,000,000—$\bar{\text{M}}$

N.B. A dash line above the numeral multiplies the value by 1,000: M$\bar{\text{V}}$ = 4,000.

For the use of Roman numerals in outlines, *see* page 77.

CHAPTER SEVEN

Spelling and Choosing Words

Rules for Spelling

Rules and examples that follow are those commonly accepted. However, there are exceptions to many rules so that a writer who is in doubt should check words in an authoritative dictionary.

Dictionaries should also be compared in their listing for alternate forms. For example, Webster's explains that when another spelling or form is joined to the entry word by the word *also*, the spelling following it is a variant, less commonly used; when the entry is followed by the word *or* and then another spelling, the two forms or spellings are equally acceptable in standard practice:

woolly *also* wooly   gases *also* gasses (n. pl.)
canceled *or* cancelled   labeled *or* labelled

Final Consonants

1. With monosyllables and words accented on the last syllable when ending with a single consonant preceded by a single vowel double the consonant (other than *w*, *x*, or *y*) before a suffix beginning with a vowel.

bag	baggage	plan	planned
begin	beginning	refer	referring
bid	bidden	remit	remittance
equip	equipped	sad	sadden
impel	impelled	sit	sitting
man	mannish	wed	wedded
occur	occurred	wit	witty

Exceptions

infer	inferable, *but:* inferred, inferring
transfer	transferable, *but:* transferring, transferred

2. Final consonants when preceded by two vowels are not doubled in adding a suffix beginning with a vowel.

beat	beaten
congeal	congealing
retail	retailing
soak	soaking

3. Final consonants are not doubled when the word ends in more than one consonant.

conform	conformed	conforming
help	helped	helping

4. Final consonants may or may not be doubled when the accent is thrown forward. The American tendency is not to double the final consonant, British usage is to double it.

benefit	benefiting *or* benefitting, benefited *or* benefitted
cancel	canceling *or* cancelling, canceled *or* cancelled
travel	traveling *or* travelling, traveled *or* travelled

5. Adjectives ending with *l*, like other adjectives, add *ly* to form the corresponding adverbs.

accidentally	exceptionally	occasionally
casually	finally	really
coolly	legally	unusually

Prefixes and suffixes ending in *ll* generally drop one *l* in combination.

already	always
although	helpful
altogether	wonderful

6. Words ending in *n* keep that letter before the suffix *ness.*

barrenness	meanness
greenness	plainness
keenness	suddenness

7. Words ending in a double consonant usually retain both consonants before suffixes.

assess	assessment	shrill	shrilly
embarrass	embarrassment	success	successful

Final E

8. Words ending in silent *e* usually omit the *e* before suffixes beginning with a vowel.

abridging	encouraging	pleasing
acknowledging	forcible	salable
arguing	giving	subduing
arrival	guidance	tracing
blamable	hoping	truism
changing	judging	typing
coming	lovable	using
deplorable	loving	wiring
desirable	managing	writing
dining	mistaking	

9. When words end in soft *ce* or *ge*, keep the *e* before *able* and *ous.*

advantageous	noticeable
changeable	outrageous
chargeable	peaceable
courageous	pronounceable
enforceable	serviceable
manageable	traceable

10. Keep final *e* in the present participle of *singe, tinge, dye.*

dyeing	singeing
eyeing	tingeing

11. When words end in *oe*, keep the *e* before a suffix beginning with any vowel except *e*.

canoeing
hoeing
toeing

12. When words end in silent *e*, keep the *e* before a suffix beginning with a consonant.

baleful   management
encouragement   movement
extremely   ninety
lonely   useful
lovely

Exceptions

acknowledgment   duly
argument   judgment
            truly

13. Verbs ending in *ie* change the termination to *y* before adding *ing*.

die dying (*but*, died)   lie lying (*but*, lied)
        tie tying (*but*, tied)

Final Y

14. Words ending in *y* preceded by a consonant change *y* to *i* before a suffix, unless the suffix begins with *i*.

busy   busier   business
defy   defiant   defies
mercy   merciful   merciless

But

carry   carrying
hurry   hurrying
study   studying
thirty   thirtyish

15. Words ending in *y* preceded by a vowel generally keep the *y* before a suffix.

buyer	buying
delayed	delaying
obey	obeying

Exceptions

daily	paid
laid	said

16. Monosyllabic adjectives usually keep *y* when adding a suffix.

dry	dryly
sly	slyly

17. Follow the well-known rhyme in spelling words in *ie* and *ei*.

I before E
Except after C
Or when sounded as A
As in n**ei**ghbor and w**ei**gh

ei used after *c*

ceiling	deceit	receipt
conceive	perceive	receive

ie used after all letters except *c*

achieve	fiend	niece	shriek
apiece	frontier	pierce	sieve
believe	grief	relieve	yield
chief	mischief	reprieve	

Exceptions

counterfeit	forfeit	leisure	seize
foreign	height	neither	weird

ei sounded as *a*

feign	reign
heinous	their
neighbor	weight

Words Ending in C

18. Words ending with a vowel plus *c* remain unchanged before *a, o, u,* or a consonant.

frolicsome   critical

Before an added *e, i,* or *y,* the letter *k* is inserted if the *c* sound remains hard.

frolicked   panicky

Nothing is added after *c* if the *c* sound becomes soft.

criticism   toxicity

19. Words ending with a consonant plus *c* usually remain unchanged before any suffix, but occasionally an inserted *k* is found: usually *arc, arced, arcing,* but sometimes *arcked, arcking.*

Words Ending in S or S-Sounds

20. When words end in *s* or an *s*-sound (*ss, x, ch, sh, z*), the plural is formed by adding *es* to the singular.

annex   annexes
church   churches
dish   dishes
hostess   hostesses
quartz   quartzes

Variations in American and British Spelling

21. Note the variations in American and British usage in the following:
(1) Words ending in *or.*

American	British	American	British
arbor	arbour	humor	humour
behavior	behaviour	labor	labour
candor	candour	misdemeanor	misdemeanour
clamor	clamour	neighbor	neighbour
endeavor	endeavour	odor	odour
favor	favour	parlor	parlour

flavor	flavour	rumor	rumour
harbor	harbour	vigor	vigour
honor	honour		

Note that *discoloration, horror, invigorate, mirror, pallor, tenor, terror,* and *tremor* do not take *u* in British spelling.

Note that adjectives formed from *clamor, humor, labor, odor, rigor,* and *vigor* do not take *u* in British spelling.

clamorous	laborious	rigorous
humorous	odorous	vigorous

(2) Words ending in *er.*

American	*British*	*American*	*British*
center	centre	meter	metre
maneuver	manoeuvre	reconnoiter	reconnoitre

(3) Words ending in *ise* and *ize.*

Most words ending in this sound take *ize.* Some may be spelled either *ize* or *ise.* American usage generally prefers *ize.*

The following spellings are those given in Webster's:

advise	compromise	exercise	patronize
amortize	demoralize	extemporize	penalize
anglicize	despise	familiarize	recognize
apologize	devise	fertilize	satirize
authorize	disfranchise	franchise	scrutinize
baptize	disorganize	harmonize	specialize
capitalize	dramatize	merchandise	supervise
centralize	economize	mobilize	surmise
characterize	emphasize	modernize	surprise
chastise	enterprise	monetize	sympathize
civilize	equalize	naturalize	utilize
colonize	excise	organize	visualize

Using the Dictionary

When you are unsure of the spelling of a word, you may find it difficult to locate the word in the dictionary. English spelling is confusing because many letters and combinations of letters sound a good deal alike. The solution is to try the various possible equivalents for each sound you hear when you say the word.

Pronounce the word slowly and divide it into syllables. List the possible spellings for each syllable by consulting the following chart.

General sound	Examples	Approximate Equivalents
long a (ā)	mate, lain, gay, reign feign, bouquet, whey cliché	a, ai, ay, ei ei, et, ey, é
broad a (ä) or circumflex o (ô)	father, pause, qualm foster, bought	a, au, al o, ough
long e (ē)	cedar, seek feat, ceiling, yield	e, ee ea, ei, ie
f	flee, laugh, phobia	f, gh, ph
long i (ī)	aisle, pile, stein, high, lye	i, ei, ai, igh, ye
short i (ĭ)	depict, embryonic	i, y
j	jet, page, ledge	j, ge, dge
k	pike, capital, bisque	k, c, que
long o (ō)	dome, roam	o, oa
ow	flower, about	ow, ou
r	rate, wrist	r, wr
s	cost, descent, rice	s, sc, ce
sh	shoe, chute, suspicion, conscience, mission, elation	sh, ch ci, sci ssi, ti
z	amazing, surmise	z, s

You should also check the following parts of suffixes that sound alike: -able and -ible; -ant and -ent; -ance and -ence; -cial and -tial; -cious and -tious; -osity and -ocity.

Remember, too, that a consonant is usually doubled only after a short vowel sound (a, e, i, o, u) as in planning, repellent, imminent, allotting, rebuttal.

Suppose you wanted to look up cynosure. The word would begin with either s or c. The long i sound could be i, ei, or y. The rest of the word would probably be -nosure. You would try si, sei, and sy, ci, and cei without finding the word, but cy would bring success.

Similarly, *idiosyncrasy* contains several possible combinations. Thinking of *ideology,* you would try *ideo,* perhaps, as well as *idio.* The next syllable could be *sin, syn, cin,* or *cyn,* and the last two syllables might be *cracy, crasy, krasy,* or *kracy.* Of course, you will generally find the word before you reach the last syllable, but a systematic approach will help you to analyze a word and shorten the search.

Choosing the Correct Word

When choosing the word that best expresses the intent, some writers and speakers mistake one word for another similar one. Note the differences in the pairs and groups of words that follow.

For lively discussions of the misuse of words, see *The Elements of Style* by William Strunk, Jr., and E. B. White (Macmillan), *The Careful Writer* and other books by Theodore M. Bernstein (Atheneum), *The Writer's Art* by James J. Kilpatrick (Andrews, McMeel & Parker Inc.), *On Language* by William Safire (Times Books), and *On Writing Well* by William Zinsser (Harper & Row).

Words Often Confused

accede	to adhere to an agreement
exceed	to surpass
accept	to receive
except	to exclude
adherence	attachment
adherents	followers
adapt	to adjust
adept	proficient
addition	something added
edition	the whole number of copies published at one time
adverse	opposed
averse	disinclined

affect (vb.)	to influence, to change
effect	to accomplish (vb.); result (n.)
afterward, afterwards	both forms are correct
all right	the correct form
alright	no such spelling
all ready	entirely ready (The work is *all ready* for you.)
already	action has occurred (I have *already* finished the work.)
all together	in a body (The family is *all together.*)
altogether	entirely (You are *altogether* right.)
allude	to refer to indirectly
refer	to mention something definitely
allusion	an indirect reference
delusion	an error of judgment
illusion	an error of vision
almost (adv.)	nearly
most	an adj., an adv. of comparison, a pronoun: most people, most beautiful, most of them
altar (n.)	a sacred place of worship
alter (vb.)	to change
amateur	one who engages in a pursuit, study, science, sport as a pastime
novice	one new in a business or in a profession
amoral	nonmoral
immoral	dissolute
unmoral	having no moral perception; synonymous with nonmoral
among	use *among* when reference is to more than two
between	use *between* when reference is made to only two persons

amount	bulk, the sum total referring to number
number	refers to something counted
quantity	refers to something measured
anecdote	a narrative of a particular incident
antidote	a remedy to counteract poison
anywhere	no such word as *anywheres*
appraise	to value
apprise	to inform, to notify
apprize	to put a value on; seldom used, same as *appraise*
apt	suitable, appropriate, skilled
liable	legally bound; implies undesirable consequences
likely	possible
ascent	act of rising
assent	consent
assay	to test and to analyze, as ore; to estimate
essay (vb.)	to try, to attempt
attorney	strictly applies to one transacting legal business
lawyer	applies to anyone in the profession; also, one legally appointed by another to transact business for him
avocation	a minor occupation pursued especially for enjoyment
vocation	a regular calling or profession
balance	the difference between the debit and credit side of an account
remainder	the comparatively small part left over
berth	a place in which to sleep in a railroad sleeping car or on a ship
birth	act of being born
beside	at the side of
besides	in addition to

biannual	twice a year; synonymous with semiannual
biennial	every two years
bouillon	a clear soup
bullion	uncoined gold or silver in bars or ingots
breath (n.)	respiration
breathe (vb.)	to inhale and exhale
bring	to convey toward (the speaker)
take	to carry from (the speaker)
calender	a machine for finishing paper or cloth
calendar	record of time
cannon	a large gun
canon	a law; a rule; a clergyman belonging to the staff of a cathedral or collegiate church
canvas (n.)	strong tent cloth
canvass (vb.)	act of soliciting for orders, votes, etc.
capital	the seat of government of a state or country; money invested in a business
capitol	a building in which a state legislative body meets; with cap., the building in which the U.S. Congress meets in Washington
casual	happening by chance
causal	relating to a cause or causes
censer	an incense pan
censor	a critic; to criticize
censure	to blame
cession	the act of ceding, that is, a granting or a surrender of something, especially the transfer of territory from one country to another
session	a term or a meeting place; as of a court, legislature, or any organized assembly
character	sum of qualities that constitute the true individuality of a person
reputation	what others think of a person

cite	to summon to appear before a court, to quote by way of authority or proof, to refer to
sight	a view
site	a place
client	a person using the services of a lawyer or other professional person
customer	a person who purchases a commodity or service
close	to shut; to bring to an end
clothes	wearing apparel
cloths	fabrics
coarse	rough
course	a direction of going, action; part of a meal
colleague	an associate in a profession or a civil or ecclesiastical office
partner	a member of a partnership, joint owner in business
collision	a clash
collusion	secret agreement to defraud
commence	to begin; more formal than begin
comments	remarks
compare	to bring things together, to note points of difference or similarity
contrast	to bring things together to note points of difference
continual	frequently recurring; refers to time and implies close succession (*continual* rains)
continuous	uninterrupted; refers to time and space and implies continuity (*continuous* heartbeat)
council	an assembly or group for conference
counsel	advice, legal adviser
credible	worthy of acceptance
creditable	praiseworthy
credulous	ready to believe on uncertain evidence

customary	established by custom, conforming to common usage
habitual	according to habit
usual	frequent, ordinary
decease	death
disease	illness
device	mechanical appliance
devise	to contrive, to give by will
discredit	to destroy confidence in
disparage	to speak slightingly of, to undervalue
disinterested	lack of self-interest
uninterested	not interested, indifferent
disqualify	to render unfit
unqualified	not fitted
dying	ceasing to live
dyeing	coloring
emerge	to rise from, to come into view
immerge	to plunge into, to immerse
emigration	the moving from a country
immigration	the moving into a country
eminent	outstanding, high, lofty
imminent	threatening to happen soon
empty	having nothing in it (an empty bottle)
vacant	having nothing on it or in it (vacant land; a vacant apartment)
endorse	in America, preferred to *indorse*
envelop (vb.)	to put a covering about
envelope (n.)	a wrapper
error	an act involving a departure from truth or accuracy
mistake	a misunderstanding
exceedingly	very greatly
excessively	too greatly

exceptional	unusual
exceptionable	open to objection
excite	to stir up emotionally
incite	to stir into action
expect	to regard as likely to happen
suspect	to doubt the truth of
extant	still existing
extent	measure, length
famous	celebrated
noted	eminent, well known
notorious	unfavorably noted
few	used in reference to number
less	used in reference to quantity
flammable	synonyms meaning capable of being easily
inflammable	ignited
formally	ceremoniously
formerly	in times past
forth	forward
fourth	the next after *third*
guarantee	to secure; preferred in the verb sense
guaranty	financial security; preferred in the noun sense
hanged	of a person
hung	of an object
healthful	health-giving, as of climate
healthy	in good health
wholesome	producing a good effect, as of food
hire	to employ, to obtain the use of
lease	to grant by lease, to hold under a lease
let	to give the use of, to be let or leased
human	pertaining to mankind
humane	benevolent
hypercritical	too critical
hypocritical	insincere

imply	the speaker implies
infer	the hearer infers
impossible	not possible
impracticable	not possible under present conditions
indict (ĭn dīt′)	to charge with an offense
indite	to write, to compose and write
ingenious	clever
ingenuous	frank, naïve
lay	to set down
lie	to recline
lean	having little fat
lien	a legal claim
leave	to depart from
let	to allow, to permit
legible	easy to read
eligible	qualified to be chosen
lessee	a tenant
lessor	one who gives a lease
loose	free
loosen	to free
lose	to mislay
majority	more than half (sing. or pl., according to use)
plurality	the largest number of votes cast for one person, a greater number than any other but less than half of the votes cast
marital	pertaining to marriage
martial (mär′ shəl)	pertaining to war, military
marshal	to arrange; an official
medal	a badge of honor
meddle	to interfere
miner	a worker in a mine
minor	underage; inferior in extent, importance, or size

moral (mor′ al) (adj.)	virtuous, right, and proper
morale (mo rale′) (n.)	state of mind (the *morale* of the students)
new	recent
novel	unusual
oculist	one who treats eyes
optician	one who makes eyeglasses
optometrist	one who measures the vision
ordinance	law, prescribed practice or usage
ordnance	military supplies
overdo	to do too much
overdue	past due
partially	in some degree
partly	in part
partition	a division
petition	a formal written request, a prayer
party	a body of persons; refers to a group, not to a single person (except in law)
person	an individual
persecute	to oppress, to subject to persistent ill-treatment
prosecute	to sue
personal	individual, private
personnel	the staff of an organization
plaintiff	a party to a lawsuit
plaintive	mournful
practical	that which can be done advantageously; sensible, not theoretical (can refer to persons or things)
practicable	that which can be done; used to refer to things
precede	to go before
proceed	to begin

proposal	something offered for acceptance or rejection
proposition	something offered for discussion, assertion
respectfully	courteously
respectively	each in the order given
resume	to put on anew, to begin again
résumé	a summing up
role	a part or character in a play
roll	a list; to revolve
salary	a fixed periodical payment made to a person employed in other than manual or mechanical work
wages	workman's or servant's periodical pay
sample	a part of anything presented for inspection
specimen	a part, or one of a number, intended to show the quality of the whole
seasonable	timely, in keeping with the season
seasonal	periodical, affected by the seasons
specie	coin or coined money, usually of gold or silver
species (sing. and pl.) (spē shēz)	sort, variety
stable	firmly established, as *stable* price; barn
staple	produced regularly or in large quantities; a commodity for which the demand is constant
staid (adj.)	sedate
stayed	remained, postponed
stationary	not moving; fixed
stationery	writing material
suit	a set, as of clothes; a legal action; wooing; to please
suite	a retinue; a number of things constituting a set, series, or sequence, as a suite of rooms

talesman	a person summoned to make up the required number of jurors
talisman	a charm
tantamount	equivalent in value, meaning, or effect (His statement was *tantamount* to a confession.)
paramount	highest in rank or jurisdiction
temporal	limited by time; pertaining to the present life, distinguished from the sacred or eternal
temporary	lasting for a time only
unquestionable	indisputable
unquestioned	that which has not been questioned
waiver	the giving up of a claim
waver	to hesitate

Foreign Words and Phrases

(Selected from *The Random House Dictionary of the English Language*)

Latin Words and Phrases

annus mirabilis	Wonderful year
arbiter elegantiae	A judge in matters of taste
bona fides	Good faith
carpe diem	Enjoy the present
casus belli	A cause justifying war
causa sine qua non	An indispensable condition
cave canem	Beware of the dog
caveat emptor	Buy at your own risk
cui bono?	For whose advantage, to what end
de facto	In reality, actually existing
de gustibus non est disputandum	There is no disputing about tastes
de mortuis nil nisi bonum	Concerning the dead say nothing but good
Dei gratia	By the grace of God
Deo gratias	Thanks to God

Deo juvanti	With God's help
Deo volente (D.V.)	God willing
Deus vobiscum	God be with you
dis aliter visum	It seemed otherwise to the gods
Dominus vobiscum	The Lord be with you
dulce et decorum est pro patria mori	Sweet and seemly is it to die for one's country
ecce homo	Behold the man
ex cathedra	Officially, with authority
ex more	According to custom
facile princeps	Easily the first
fidus Achates	Faithful Achates; trusty friend
gaudeamus igitur	Let us be joyful
genius loci	The spirit of the place; guardian deity
hic et ubique	Here and everywhere
hic sepultus	Here lies buried
hinc illae lacrimae	Hence those tears
hoc anno	In this year
humanum est errare	To err is human
in extremis	At the point of death
in hoc signo vinces	By this sign you will conquer
in loco parentis	In the place of a parent
in medias res	Into the midst of things; into the heart of the matter
in omnia paratus	Prepared for all things
in perpetuum	Forever
in propria persona	In one's own person
in rerum natura	In the nature of things
in situ	In its place; in proper position
in statu quo	In the state in which it was before
in toto	Altogether; entirely
in transitu	In transit
ipso jure	By the law itself
jure divino	By divine law
jus canonicum	Canon law
justitia omnibus	Justice for all
labor omnia vincit	Labor conquers all things
laborare est orare	To work is to pray
laus Deo	Praise be to God
loco citato	In the place cited
locus in quo	Place in which
locus sigilli	The place of the seal

loquitur	He (or she) speaks
mens sana in corpore sano	A sound mind in a healthy body
meum et tuum	Mine and thine
miles gloriosus	A braggart soldier
mirabile dictu	Wonderful to say
mirabilia	Miracles
modus operandi	A mode of operating
morituri te salutamus	We who are about to die salute thee
motu proprio	Of one's own accord
multum in parvo	Much in little
mutatis mutandis	The necessary changes having been made
mutato nomine	The name having been changed
nemine contradicente	No one contradicting
nemine dissentiente	No one dissenting
nemo me impune lacessit	No one attacks me with impunity
nihil	Nothing
nil admirari	To wonder at nothing
nil desperandum	Nothing to be despaired of
nolens volens	Whether willing or not
non possumus	We are not able
nunc	Now
obiit	He died; she died
O tempora! O mores!	O times! O customs!
omnia vincit amor	Love conquers all
opere citato	In the volume cited
otium cum dignitate	Leisure with dignity
pari passu	With equal pace; without partiality
passim	Here and there
pater patriae	Father of his country
paucis verbis	In few words
pax vobiscum	Peace be with you
persona grata	An acceptable person
pleno jure	With full authority
primus inter pares	First among equals
pro bono publico	For the public good or welfare
pro Deo et ecclesia	For God and the church
pro forma	As a matter of form
pro memoria	For memory
pro tempore	Temporarily; for the time being

quantum sufficit	As much as suffices
quo animo?	With what spirit or intention?
quo Fata vocant	Whither the Fates call
quo jure?	By what right?
quo modo?	In what way?
quod erat demonstrandum	Which was to be shown
requiescat in pace	May he (or she) rest in peace
scripsit	He or she wrote (it)
sculpsit	He or she sculptured (it)
secundum	According to
semper idem	Always the same
semper paratus	Always ready
seriatim	In a series
sic passim	So throughout
sic semper tyrannis	Thus always to tyrants
sic transit gloria mundi	Thus passes away the glory of the world
sine die	Without fixing a day for future action or meeting
sine qua non	Something essential
summum bonum	The highest or chief good
suo jure	In one's own right
suo loco	In one's own or rightful place
suum cuique	To each his own
tempora mutantur, nos et mutamur in illis	Times change and we change with them
tempus fugit	Time flies
timeo Danaos et dona ferentes	I fear the Greeks even when they bear gifts
ubique	Everywhere
ut dict.	As directed
vade mecum	Go with me; companion
vae victis	Woe to the conquered
vale	Farewell
verbatim et literatim	Word for word and letter for letter

French Words and Phrases

à bon marché	At a bargain
à gauche	To the left-hand side
à propos de rien	Apropos of nothing
affaire de cœur	A love affair
au contraire	On the contrary

au fait	Expert, having practical knowledge of a thing
au revoir	Till we see each other again
autre temps, autres moeurs	Other times, other customs
avec plaisir	With pleasure
bête noire	Something that one especially dislikes or dreads
bon jour	Good day; hello
bon soir	Good evening; good night
catalogue raisonné	A classified or descriptive catalogue
c'est-à-dire	That is to say
c'est la vie	Such is life
chacun à son goût	Everyone to his own taste
chef de cuisine	Head cook
cherchez la femme	Look for the woman
compte rendu	Report, account
coup de grâce	A death blow
coûte que coûte	Cost what it may
dégagé	Unconstrained; without emotional involvement
de trop	Too much; too many
dernier ressort	The last resource
Dieu avec nous	God with us
Dieu défend le droit	God defends the right
Dieu et mon droit	God and my right
en plein jour	In full daylight, openly
en rapport	In sympathy or accord
fait accompli	An accomplished fact
femme de chambre	A chambermaid, a lady's maid
fête champêtre	An outdoor festival
garde du corps	A bodyguard
gardez la foi	Keep the faith
grand monde	The world at large; refined society
honi soit qui mal y pense	Evil be to him who evil thinks
ici on parle français	French is spoken here
jeu de mots	Play on words, pun
jeu d'esprit	A play of wit or fancy
j'y suis, j'y reste	Here I am, here I stay
le roi est mort, vive le roi	The king is dead! Long live the king!
le style, c'est l'homme	The style is the man
le tout ensemble	The whole (taken) together

lettre de cachet	A sealed or secret letter, usually containing orders for imprisonment
ma foi	Really!
mal de mer	Seasickness
mal du pays	Homesickness
matinée	Afternoon performance
mise en scène	Stage-setting; surroundings; environment
mon ami	My friend
monde	World; society
mot juste	The exact or appropriate word
moyen âge	The Middle Ages
n'est ce pas?	Isn't that so?
n'importe	It does not matter
nom de guerre	An assumed name
objet d'art	A work of art
peu de chose	A small matter
pièce de résistance	The principal meal; the principal event (of a series)
pied-à-terre	A temporary lodging
pis aller	The last resort or resource
quand même	Nevertheless
qui s'excuse, s'accuse	He who excuses himself accuses himself
raison d'état	For the good of the country
raison d'être	Reason for being
salle à manger	Dining room
sans doute	Without doubt
sans gêne	Without embarrassment
sans pareil	Without equal
sans peine	Without difficulty
sans peur et sans reproche	Without fear and without reproach
sans souci	Carefree
tant mieux	So much the better
tant pis	So much the worse
tout à fait	Entirely
tout à l'heure	Instantly
tout le monde	Everyone
voilà	See! Look!

Pronunciation

1. Many words include letters that should not be pronounced. In the following, do *not* pronounce the italicized letter:

ba*s*-relief	indi*c*tment
com*p*troller	qua*l*m
fore*h*ead	sa*l*mon
indi*c*t	vi*c*tuals

2. Many words include letters that should be pronounced and often are not. In the following, pronounce the italicized letter:

accident*a*lly	occasion*a*lly
accompan*i*ment	partic*u*larly
ar*c*tic	per*h*aps
can*d*idate	po*e*m
gen*e*rally	proba*b*ly
ge*o*graphy	re*a*lize
govern*m*ent	sev*e*ral
histo*r*y	su*r*prise
kep*t*	temper*a*ment
leng*th*	us*u*ally
libra*r*y	yeste*r*day
Niag*a*ra	

Note that the words in the following list are mispronounced because a letter or a syllable is incorrectly added:

athlete (*not* athelete)	hindrance (*not*
elm (*not* elum)	hinderance)
helm (*not* helum)	realtor (*not* realitor)
	umbrella (*not* umberella)

CHAPTER EIGHT

Signs and Symbols

´   acute accent

✳   asterisk, a mark used to denote a reference

@   at, about; as, velvet @ $10 per yd.

[ ]   brackets used to enclose matter incidental to the thought of the sentence or to enclose material not a part of the original being quoted.

˘   breve, a mark used to indicate a short vowel; as in the sound of *i* in *ill*

%   care of

∧   caret, a sign inserted below a line between words or letters to denote an incorrect omission

₃   cedilla, under a *c* (ç) to show it is pronounced like *s*

¢   cent or cents

√   check

“   ditto

÷   division

$ dollar or dollars

=   equals

°C.   degrees Celsius or Centigrade

°F.   degrees Fahrenheit

′   feet; as, 16′; also minutes; as, 6′

`   grave accent

>   greater than

∴   hence, therefore

≏   hyphen, indicated in a typed manuscript for typesetting

″   inches; as, 10′ 16″ (ten feet, sixteen inches); a dictionary mark indicating secondary accent

<   less than

158

-    macron, a mark used to indicate a long vowel; as in the sound of *i* in *ice*

—   minus

✕   a sign denoting multiplication; a sign denoting *by* in dimensions: as, 3 ft × 3 ft.; a character used instead of a signature by one unable to write his name

\#   number; as, #7; also a printing mark used to indicate a needed space

¶   paragraph

‖   parallel to

%   percent

+   plus

£   pound, as, £6 (English money)

~   tilde, a mark placed over *n* in Spanish words to denote the addition of the sound of *y*; as *cañon* pronounced *canyon*

§   a symbol meaning Section

Sources Consulted

Bates, Jefferson. *Writing with Precision.* Acropolis, 1978.

Bernstein, Theodore M. *The Careful Writer.* New York: Atheneum, 1979.

———. *Do's, Don'ts & Maybes of English Usage.* New York: Times Books, 1977.

Evans, Bergen, and Cornelia Evans. *A Dictionary of Contemporary American Usage.* New York: Random House, 1957.

Follett, Wilson. *Modern American Usage,* ed. by Jacques Barzun. New York: Hill & Wang, 1966.

Fowler, H. W. *A Dictionary of Modern English Usage,* 2d ed., rev. by Sir Ernest Gowers. New York: Oxford University Press, 1965.

Morris, William. *American Heritage Dictionary.* New York: Harper & Row, 1985.

Morris, William, and Mary Morris. *Harper Dictionary of Contemporary Usage,* 2d ed. New York: Harper & Row, 1985.

Newman, Edwin. *Strictly Speaking.* New York: Bobbs-Merrill, 1974.

Safire, William. *On Language.* New York: Times Books, 1980.

Stein, Jess, ed. *The Random House Dictionary of the English Language.* New York: Random House, 1984.

United States Government Printing Office Style Manual. Washington, D.C., 1984.

Webster's Ninth New Collegiate Dictionary. Springfield, Mass.: Merriam-Webster, 1985.

White, E. B. *Elements of Style.* New York: Macmillan, 1959.

Words into Type, 3d ed. Englewood Cliffs, N.J.: Prentice-Hall, 1974.

Zinsser, William. *On Writing Well.* New York: Harper & Row, 1980.

Index

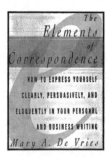